FROM BEGINNING
TO
BEGINNING

An Autobiography

by

Edward J. Levitch

1997

*I knew the wrongs and craved
the rights that should have been my birthright. The
depth of pain, suffering and hope
is engraved in each word to be read by yet another
'beginning' generation.*

EDWARD J. LEVITCH

Mad Dog
PUBLISHING COMPANY

1997

BERKELEY, CALIFORNIA

ISBN 0-9655974-0-7

Library of Congress Catalogue Card No. 96-95413

CONTENTS

ACKNOWLEDGEMENTS

As an architect and a builder over the last 34 years I have touched many peoples lives. In return I was inspired and encouraged by many. One person that stands out as a motivator to writing this book is Sally Pritchard. Sally was a neighbor when our children were growing up and my secretary until her retirement in 1991. Her words ring out today: "Why not write your story. I will help you put it down on paper." That was in 1985. And I thank her for this.

This book would never have been written without the pain of my divorce. The divorce moved me to write on. I wanted Anita, my former wife and the mother of our four sons, to understand me. I felt that through her understanding of me, even after the divorce, would help our children know us both better. This I felt to be important for their growing up and development.

Bob and Fran Rowe, my colleagues and neighbors, who watched my development in the city of Berkeley since 1958 have contributed to this book the most supportive suggestions. Fran, an author in her own right, and Bob, an architect and historian whose own family suffered the ravages of the war, offered compassionate comments that have greatly influenced this book.

Beyond this I thank my editors, Alice Shepherd and Ann Bornstein. Their contribution and encouragement made this work really happen. Ann, a close friend, has invested innumerable hours of patient reading and rereading the manuscript. She produced the final copy of this book and I express my sincere gratitude for her dedication and commitment.

The production of this book must be credited to a tireless artist, graphic artist and actor, Wayne Pope, who worked patiently with the publisher to produce a book that will touch people's hearts and minds.

INTRODUCTION

When I started writing my biography I was 61 years old. My relation to my children was shaky. My desire for them to know me better was very strong. I felt that they would benefit from my life's stories compressed into a book. I also believed that if these were stories of their father's experiences in his own words and in his own lifetime they would welcome it. As an amateur author, the time that I devoted to writing was limited. Ultimately, I completed memoirs of my entire history to the present. This book covers the period of my life up to the time that I settled permanently in the United States.

I hope that I may become an inspiration to other parents to tell their stories to their children. By doing this we contribute to new generations the unmistakable link that humans appear to need to their past.

May this book be a window into the twentieth century and may the lessons learned there be a window into the future. In this way, may we prevent what happened from happening again and again.

FROM BEGINNING TO BEGINNING:
THE JOURNEY

1. Journey begins at Beograd
2. From Beograd to Vrnacka Banja
3. From Vrnacka back to Beograd
4. From Beograd to Arandelovac
5. From Arandelovac to Mladenovac
6. From Mladenovac to Tito Uzice
7. From Tito Uzice to Krsanje
8. From Krsanje to Tito Uzice
9. From Tito Uzice to Skopje
10. From Skopje to Tirane
11. From Tirane to Durazzo
12. From Durazzo to Korcula
13. From Korcula to Split

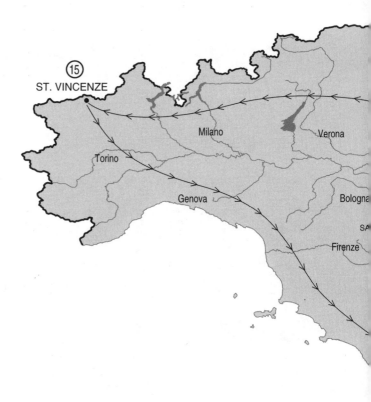

ST. VINCENZE

Milano

Verona

Torino

Genova

Bologna

SA

Firenze

14. From Split to Trieste
15. From Trieste to St. Vincenze
16. From St. Vincenze to Feramonte
    Internment Camp
17. From Reggio di Calabria to Taranto
18. From Taranto to Lece
19. From Lece to Naples

To U.S.A. aboard the
Liberty Ship Henry Gibbons

(14) TRIESTE

nezia

From
SPLIT

ITALY

★ Rome

NAPLES (19)

(18)
LECE

TARANTO
(17)

FERAMONTE INTERNMENT CAMP

Palermo

(16)
REGGIO di Calabria

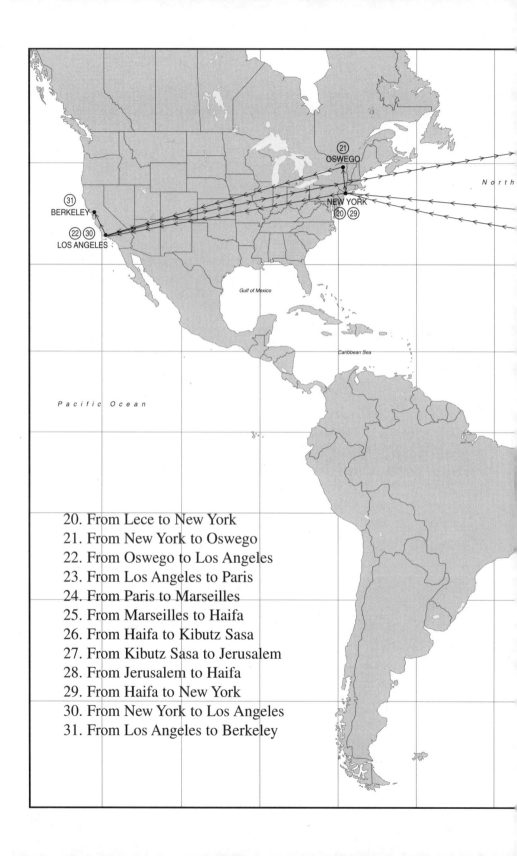

20. From Lece to New York
21. From New York to Oswego
22. From Oswego to Los Angeles
23. From Los Angeles to Paris
24. From Paris to Marseilles
25. From Marseilles to Haifa
26. From Haifa to Kibutz Sasa
27. From Kibutz Sasa to Jerusalem
28. From Jerusalem to Haifa
29. From Haifa to New York
30. From New York to Los Angeles
31. From Los Angeles to Berkeley

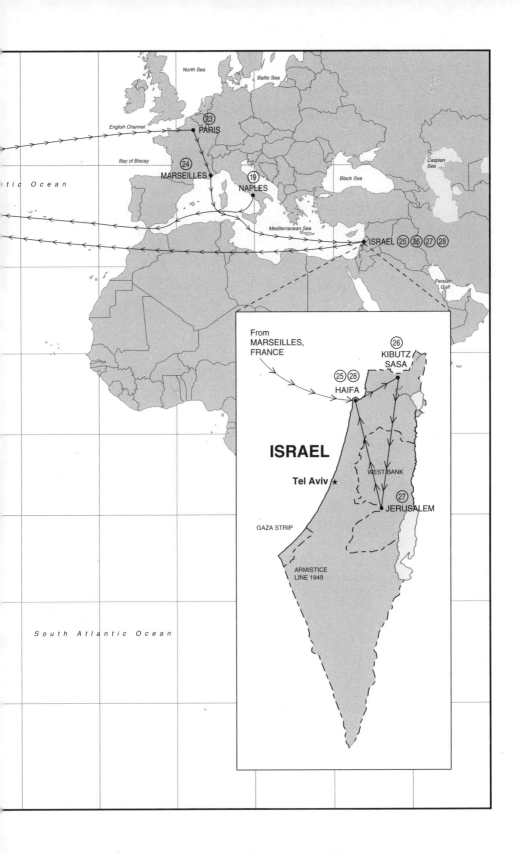

I

BEGINNINGS

In my family, we all had difficult beginnings. My mother was a very bright and intelligent woman. During the First World War, she was employed by the British Army in Greece and was in charge of an administrative division. She grew apart from her family because she excelled in her work and because she wanted to study and go to the university. Her father, who grew up during the Turkish-Ottoman rule when women had no right to self determination, prevented her from studying. When she was twenty-four, she married my father, Josif Levi, a self-determined man of twenty-five, a graduate of the University of Geneva in Switzerland, an intellectual, a pharmacist, and a poet. Her great hopes for advancement were doomed. My father, though a cultured man, was brought up in a period of male supremacy and did not allow her to take advancement courses or even piano lessons. He locked his library shelves so that she could not read his books. Heaven forbid that she might become learned! Learning was for men alone and not for women. "Como ceria estudiar. Papa no me descho," she would say in Ladino. "How I wanted to study, but Papa didn't let me." We grew up surrounded by her resentment. My father's unwillingness to give her the opportunity to learn was a heavy burden for her to carry. Still, my parents sought advancement and learning for their children, and we learned that knowledge was valuable.

My father's side of the family came from peasant stock, village folks, as they were. My great-grandfather was a cobbler. That is all I know about him, except that he had a son, David, who came to Belgrade from the town of Pirot in Serbija in search of work. Penniless, as my father told the story, my grandfather sat one day on a street bench wondering what to do. Just then a man passed by who recognized his "intelligent face" and asked him if he needed work. The man was an owner of a "Menjacka Banka," a money exchange bank. Those banks were really just tiny stores offering to exchange foreign money for local currency. My grandfather accepted that job and learned the business so well that he later opened his own bank called "Kolonijalna Banka." The bank thrived and soon my grandpa involved three of his sons in the banking business. My uncles Maurice, Isak, and Solomon became his partners. They had no formal education in banking, but they were intelligent and hard working.

My grandfather was married twice. My father was the product of my grandfather's second marriage. Miriam was my grandmother. We used to call her Baba Gigi, "gigi" meaning "giddyap," because she used to ride a horse, I think, or maybe it was because we had a picture of her riding a camel when she visited what was then Palestine. Grandma was a stately woman. We all loved her. She was the mainstay of the Levi clan of Belgrade. There were aunts, uncles, grandparents, and cousins all over the place. After our family moved to the village of Mirjevo, there were frequent family parties in our garden. There was much singing and dancing and lots of good food.

My father, Josif Levi, was born in 1897 in Belgrade, then the capital of Serbia. We used to call him Cale which was a diminutive for Father in Serbian. He had no interest in banking. Therefore, at the age of 19, before the end of the First World War, he was sent to Switzerland to study. There he learned French. He was the only son out of seven to get a higher education. He became a pharmacist and returned to Belgrade, which had become the capital of Yugoslavia as a result of the League of Nations' peace settlement.

My mother, Fortuné Jacoel, was born in Salonica, Greece in 1900. She was educated in a Catholic French school. At the age of 22, her father brought her to the resort town of Vrnjacka

Banja, Yugoslavia, for a vacation. Vrnjacka Banja was well known throughout Europe. It was the source of mineral water desired by many, including my father. It was there that he met my mother at the very well spring of the mineral water they had both come to enjoy.

After they met, my father's father (Deda) went to Fortuné's father to announce that Josif was madly in love with Fortuné and that Josif wanted to see her in Belgrade. My grandfather said that Josif had threatened to kill himself if Fortuné did not come to Belgrade. That was a traditional way of getting what you wanted. My mother's father really had no choice but to oblige. The few brief words exchanged between my father and mother in French when they met at Vrnjacka Banja had been enough for them to become engaged. The French language, which suggested culture and learning on the part of those who spoke it, probably added to Fortuné's infatuation with Josif. Their common languages were French and Ladino, neither of which were their native tongues.

So it came to pass that these two wonderful people, who hardly knew each other, became my parents. If there is anything to be learned from this, it is perhaps the notion that it is important that lovers at least want similar things from life. My parents did not. The circumstances that kept them together taught them how to coexist and, at times, even how to love. The disparity of their personalities took away from their intimacy, Father always reaching out and Mother always withholding. Father was open, sincere, and totally aware of his mortality while Mother was stoic, brave and invincible.

I know the pain my father endured when denied the opportunity to think and feel in unison with my mother. They paid the price of entering into a relationship that did not allow them to touch each other's hearts. Would we, the children, or the universe for that matter, have been better served if their match had been perfect? Perhaps yes. On the other hand, would I be who I am now? Since everything has a reason, the answer to this question is moot. We are better off for the diverse qualities we inherit from each of our parents. In my family, we all seem to have inherited the warmth and sweetness of our father and the aloofness of our mother. As it turned out, it was Mother, and not Father, who was able to take action. She was the one who later saved us from the jaws of the SS troopers.

Although Mother had not been allowed the luxury of advanced study, learning was admired and encouraged by her. In a sense, I think our mother encouraged us more than our father did. Since she could not learn, her children would.

I was the oldest. We were all born in Belgrade, Serbia. The fall of the Austrian-Hungarian monarchy had led. by the end of 1918, to the formal establishment of the Kingdom of the Serbs, Croats, and Slovenes. The name was changed in September, 1931 to Yugoslavia. This was a unification of the Kingdom of Serbia, which had included Macedonia since 1912, with the provinces of southern Austria-Hungary which were inhabited by Slovenes, Croats, and Serbs. The Kingdom of Montenegro was incorporated into the new state. Croatia, Bosnia and Montenegro were not enthusiastic about this development because they felt that they were losing their national independence.

I was born on September 5, 1924, Leon on July 9, 1927, and sister Manon on August 29, 1931. I was named David after my grandfather but my nickname was Edi and to this day I don't know where that name came from. We were all intelligent and healthy children. At a very young age, I felt the stress between my parents and I suffered. We spoke mainly French at home. We learned Serbian on the street and in school. I believe that this language issue contributed to the less than clear communication between Father and children and between Mother and children. They even used Ladino, a jargon of Spanish, Serbian and Hebrew, when they wanted to keep their conversations private. We picked up some of it as we grew up. This was the political and personal climate in which we were delivered. The national stress coupled with great personal differences between our parents must have affected our entire family. It is a small wonder that we did not turn into total misfits or dysfunctional products of a dysfunctional family.

I was a very sensitive child. I remember well the pain when one day I was told by my parents that I had to see a psychiatrist. There and then I was pronounced "crazy." The stigma attached to psychiatry in those days was very serious. I became self-conscious, and the day I was supposed to go, I climbed up on the roof of our house to hide so that I could not be taken to the psychiatrist. I never found out what was wrong with me, but I felt ashamed. I fought back and that made matters worse. I was the "ijo malo," the bad son. No matter how hard I tried to be good, I was the "ijo malo."

My elementary school education began in a tiny one room school house in the village of Mirjevo, just six kilometers out of central Belgrade. My childhood before the age of seven is somewhat foggy. I remember that I was not a happy child. My social life in Belgrade during my childhood was limited. My mother tongue was French, and since I didn't really start speaking Serbian until I entered school at the age of seven, I felt pretty isolated from my peers.

My Mother seems to have set herself apart, probably because she spoke no Serbian at all. In retrospect, I think that her residual Greek "historical sophistication", coupled with the intellectual Western attitude that she developed during the First World War continued her bent toward the western culture. She arranged to have us meet French children of "a higher class" of French visitors to Belgrade. My mother was the driving force for education in our family. She insisted that we learn how to write in French. I was a poor speller and this caused her consternation. Also, she had beautiful handwriting, while I was somewhat sloppy. She reprimanded me for this frequently. I doubt that my parents knew how I was hurting because I was estranged from my native culture. My mother's ever proper Greek attitude about everything caused my Serbian father a great deal of suffering. I had an uncle, Uncle Avram, who also married a Greek woman. He, too, had a difficult marriage. I remember my father and my uncle speaking about that at times. Their only son, Diko, also had difficulty in growing up. I believe that the personality differences and attitudes between the Greeks and the Serbs were significant and that Serbia was not an ideal melting pot for them.

I was about eight years old when we moved to Mirjevo. Our house was a very simple structure that my father designed and built while we still lived in the apartment in Belgrade. I did not have much of a chance to watch the building process. After we moved, my father and I built a garden gazebo, a front porch, a brick fence, and a bathroom addition. Because we had no work-shop, we sometimes worked in the living room. I remember building a beautiful credenza with my father there.

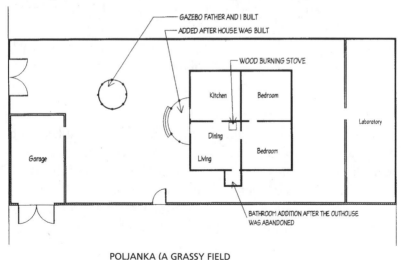

Sketch of Site & Floor Plan of my Childhood Home

I completed elementary school at the age of ten in the spring of 1935. My years in that one room schoolhouse can best be described as four years of torture. Mercifully, there were some rewards and small pleasures that I remember about that period. There was the "poljanka" playing field where we played soccer, and there were my friends Nidja, his brother Milan, and my Jewish friend Niski, whose real name was Nisim.

When I was about 12, I learned to do masonry work. I liked working with my father, especially building a laboratory in the back yard where Father installed various machines for manufacturing cosmetics. He imported a German tableting machine, a toothpaste blender, and a toothpaste tube filler. The toothpaste he manufactured was called "Biser," which means pearl in Serbian. He manufactured mothballs called Naftalin, birth control products called Alpha, and a variety of perfumes, colognes, and creams. Father owned and operated his drug store, known as "Drogerija Levic," on Uzunmirkova Ulica No. 5 in Belgrade. He was a pharmacist of some renown, educated in Switzerland, a master of his trade. He was called Doctor by all his friends. Common ailments were treated with medications prescribed by doctors and handmade, with poetic license, by pharmacists. That was a happy period in his life and in mine.

I enjoyed working with my father in the laboratory for the next couple of years. I tended to the machines including a water distilling machine. Distilled water was used extensively by druggists, and my father was a their chief supplier. One day, when I was fourteen, I decided to deliver a jug of distilled water from the laboratory to the drugstore by car. Father had left me the car keys to fix a flat tire. I had no driver's license and was careful not to be caught by the police. A double pillow on the seat gave me height, an old hat gave me age, and sun glasses covered my childish face. I thought nothing of driving six kilometers through the city streets with a jug of distilled water and my little brother Leon in the back seat. While I was on the way to the store, Mother called our housekeeper and learned that I had gone by car to the store. Her face pale with fear, she rushed to father to report my action. However, when we arrived safely, she protected me from my father's wrath.

I entered Realna Gimnazija, a junior high school for men in the fall of 1935, and then I met my first love, Nelika. She lived across the street and usually took the same streetcar to go to her school, the Shesta Gimnazija for women. Realna Gimnazija, which we called Realka, was near Kalimegdan, a major city park in Belgrade. My secret love for Nelika called for creativity in devising means of encountering each other. A spy hole drilled through the mortar of our brick fence made my departure coincide "accidentally" with her appearance each day. Hand in hand, we would go to the street car. Once we even arranged to go to Kalimegdan Park. I will never forget that ecstatic experience: we held hands and we gazed at each other. Nelika's family had its share of problems. Nelika's mother, who was Jewish, was married before the war to a man of German descent. The Yugoslav partisans executed him after the war. They assumed that all people of German descent had cooperated with the German Nazis, although the family knew that he never had.

When I was only twelve years old I began to feel anger and hatred for the Germans who were killing the Jewish people. I had my Bar Mitzvah in 1937, four years after Hitler came to power. I spent days glued to the radio listening to Hitler's speeches. We all thought that the radio would break from the hysteria and shouting at the microphone. We were petrified listening to the threats that he was making. No one believed that he would carry them out, but one by one, he did. Gradually, I transferred all my anger from my parents and my school to the Germans. This was a relief because I did not want to be angry with my parents. I wanted to be loved by them, and I wanted to love them.

I graduated at the age of 14, in 1939, only a few years after Hitler's overt persecution of the Jews began. For the next two years I drifted without a goal agonizing over the injustices we heard about. My father gave me work in his laboratory and in the pharmacy. There was talk about my entering the school of commerce. My Uncle Jacques even suggested that I might study architecture. Mainly I was preoccupied with news of persecutions of our Jewish people in Germany and with the Blitzkrieg in Poland and Czechoslovakia. Even though the country was in turmoil, I enjoyed the violin lessons that my parents afforded me and I was told that I was talented. That was the one time that I can remember being encouraged by my father.

The period in Yugoslavian history between 1937 and 1941 was one of continuous upheaval and political maneuvering. Old traditional hatreds between the small nations of Croatia, Slovenia, Serbia, Bosnia, and Montenegro were put aside for the moment. The biggest issue at that time was the question of which of the major powers would offer the most preferential treatment in case of a major conflagration. Hitler's plan to be a grand master of Europe and Russia took into account the necessity to preserve the breadbasket in the Balkans. Promises were made by Mussolini to Hitler that Yugoslavia would sign the Tripartite Agreement in exchange for the Greek port of Salonica and that war with Yugoslavia could be averted. This agreement would guarantee Yugoslavian cooperation and support for the German war machine. The Tripartite Agreement was signed on March 25, 1941.

The Serbian people were vehemently opposed to any cooperation with the Nazis. Two days after the signing of the agreement, there was a coup d'etat, called the Putsch, which toppled Prime Minister Cevetkovic from power. It was led by Milan Grol, the leader of the Democratic Party. On March 27, 1941, I took to the streets. I was 16 years old. I waved the Yugoslav flag on Terazije, a public plaza in Belgrade. The fervor of the Yugoslav youth could not be inhibited. We chanted anti-Nazi songs and broke the show windows of the German travel agency. We threw Hitler's bust on the street and burned the German flag. Little did we know what the effect of our actions would be. I doubted that anyone cared. We were carried away by our anger for Mr. Cvetkovic, the ousted Prime Minister of Yugoslavia. We heard Hitler say on the radio that Belgrade would float in its own blood for rejecting the agreement and for the people's actions on the streets of Belgrade. Father gathered the entire family together in expectation of a reprisal. He drove us to safety to stay in a hotel in Vrnjacka Banja while he returned to Belgrade to fulfill his military obligation. His duty as a pharmacist was to establish a field hospital in the center of town.

A week later, the reprisal really happened. On Sunday morning, April 6, 1941, Hitler's planes, dive bombers called stukas, killed 30,000 people in the city of Belgrade. My father's survival of the bombing was a miracle in itself. His description of that day was that it was sheer hell. He did not go into detail except to say that the sound of the diving bombers was absolutely deafening. The Yugoslavian government had no chance to respond in any way. It capitulated ten days later. My father must have been clairvoyant to have taken us to Vrnjacka Banja a week earlier. After hearing Hitler's speeches on the radio, everybody should have been clairvoyant.

The next day we left Vrnjacka Banja on the road to an unknown destination and into hiding, I was clutching my violin and dreamt of having to use it to earn a living to support our family in exile. Maybe it was only natural for me to think of supporting my family through my violin playing, as it was the one activity of mine which my parents admired very much.

Top left to right: Aunt Bukiza, Uncle Maurice, Aunt Laura, Uncle Avram
Middle left to right: Grandpa David with grandson, a Relative, My Grandma Baba Gigi,
a Relative with daughter.
Bottom left to right: Nelika and Mimi, cousins, daughters of Aunt Bukitsa
and Uncle Maurice. 1934 Belgrade.

Sister Manon, Brother Leon, Myself, Mother and Father. 1940 Belgrade.

My Grandfather David's tombstone in Belgrade, Yugoslavia

Grandma Baba Gigi with cousin Diko, Uncle Isak's son.

Myself with Mother (center) and Uncle Isak (right)

Our dog Dijana with family on the "Poljanka" (the green turf) and our car a Willis 77; our Belgrade home is in background. Approx. 1935

Top left to right:
Uncle Isak, Aunt Elsa,
Uncle Solomon, Aunt
Laura & Uncle Zak.
Mid row:
My Father, Grandmother
& Mother holding me
on her lap.
Small fry in foreground,
surrounding another rela-
tive.

On a trip to Smederevo,
the wine country near
Belgrade. The valiant car
on the right.
Approx. 1934

II

IN HIDING

At midnight on the day of the bombing of Belgrade, my father returned to us. He told us incredible stories: how the deafening sounds of the stukas, the whistling dive bombers, had terrified the civilian population and how his little American car, a Willys 77, pulled through the bomb craters and the rubble of the bombed out buildings. He survived because his car had been requisitioned by two Yugoslav officers who ordered him at gunpoint to drive them out of Belgrade. He told the officers that his family was in Vrnjacka Banja and, if they would not mind, he would like to pick up his wife and children. They agreed. This moved him away from the German blitzkrieg. When Father arrived, he was totally devastated. He had some rest, and an hour later we left Vrnjacka Banja. The two officers and the five of us, Father, Mother, sister Manon, brother Leon, and myself, packed into the small four-passenger car to go to Uzice, southwest of Belgrade. The little car took it well. We knew that it had been made by people who would liberate us and free us from German hordes of murderers. We loved our little car. I took care of it, washed and polished it every time I had a chance, and I had learned to drive it while sitting on my father's lap.

We arrived in Uzice early in the morning. The two officers were grateful to my father for driving, and we were most thankful to them for allowing my father to take the entire family along. None of us had been in Uzice before. All of Uzice was in a panic over what happened to Belgrade. Everybody stayed glued to the radios to hear the latest news, but without success. The Belgrade radio station was out. News traveled only through the grapevine.

We soon found a room. It was not very clean, I remember. My mother could not tolerate dirt or bugs. Without much ado, she boiled water and we scrubbed the wood plank floor. It was beautiful when we were done, almost white, with natural wood grain showing through. My father went out to gather what news he could, and just as we were settling in, he returned with his report: the Germans were closing in and were about to encircle Uzice. The Yugoslav army had not been able to mount an effective resistance to the Germans and plans were being made to surrender. Father thought it best that he and I should leave Mother, Manon, and Leon in Uzice, and that we should go into hiding. We hugged each other and Father and I left. There was no time to think about what our departure could mean. We were irrational and impulsive, as if the debacle of the Yugoslav army had transferred to us. We had no plan for our immediate or distant future.

There was only a small amount of gasoline in the tank of our car. We drove for about an hour and reached the top of a hill, just outside a village. From there, we could see a division of German Panzer tanks, guns, and troop carriers traveling without any opposition. We stopped. Father decided that was the end of the road for us. There was no point in trying to return to our family by car. First, there was not enough gasoline, and second, we could be killed by the Germans if they overtook us on the road. So that the car would not fall into German hands, we pushed it over the hill into a huge ravine, some one hundred feet below. We watched the car disintegrate as it blew up. We gave up our impulsive attempt to escape and began our trek back to Uzice on foot to reunite with Mother, Leon, and Manon.

It was late evening and darkness fell upon us. It was a good time to be on the road. The ditches on the side of the road protected us. Father and I jumped into them whenever anything sounded or moved anywhere near us. Ultimately, we went off the road for safety. Father buried his military issue revolver for fear of being shot or imprisoned by the Germans if we were to be captured. About midnight, after a six-hour walk, we came upon an empty barn. We climbed up to the hayloft and fell into a deep sleep. All we had with us were the clothes on our back, and none of them were waterproof. It started raining and the barn roof was not waterproof either. The chilly rain soaked our clothes, and, when we woke up, we could barely move. Nevertheless, we forced ourselves. Slowly, with our bones and muscles aching at every step, we walked through the open country. We reached Uzice in the afternoon.

Mother was very happy to see us back. She hugged and kissed us both and then heated water on the stove. We soaked in a round metal tub made to fit a human body sitting with legs crossed. The next day, Father went out and, before the Germans entered the town, he arranged to take us to the mountains into hiding.

Mother had sewn a few Napoleon gold pieces into a coat-lining. Father used them to interest a young Serbian peasant into leading us to a tiny village where his parents lived, high in the Black Mountains between Uzice and Sarajevo. The village was called Krsanje. To get there we had to walk across the countryside for two nights and one day. The six of us moved along wearily, with all of our family's earthly possessions on our backs. Single file, up steep mountain ranges and over occasional valley floors, higher and higher we climbed. Suddenly, Krsanje was before us, two or three wooden cabins, an outhouse, and a flour mill.

Our leader and protector was a clever person. He and Father came up with a plan. He would introduce my father to his father as his uncle, his father's own brother who had been lost during the first World War. My father's name became Milutin. We caught our guide's family by surprise. They knew nothing of the war and even less about us, but in the true tradition of Serbian hospitality, they received us all with open arms. We worked together and ate together as a family. Our sleeping quarters consisted of a single cabin, approximately seven feet by seven feet. It rested precariously on a few rocks. Our mattresses consisted of straw filled bags. There were wall-to-wall bags and people, but we were free! The Germans would never know of this place.

I tilled the rocky soil with the village folk. Together, we carried the sacks of wheat to the village mill, run by a stream emanating from mountains even higher than ours. The soil was hard and dry and not very fertile.

It was Fall of 1941. The Germans had settled in the major cities of Yugoslavia. Our country had fallen as had many others. There was now no stopping the German war machine. Our daily activities consisted of working on the terraced soil, cultivating the ground in preparation for spring planting. The women were tending to the chores of preparing food for the hard working men. After some four months we started asking about access to Belgrade. We discovered that, by taking a four-hour walk through almost impassable mountain ravines, man and donkey could reach a railroad station from which one could get a train to Belgrade. I was the brave one and decided to attempt the trip. I was 16 years old then. I felt old enough to tell my parents that I wanted to return to Belgrade to find my uncles and aunts and particularly my grandmother Baba Gigi. To accomplish this, I donned my peasant clothing including some "opanke," leather shoes with unicorn-like fronts. I looked just like a native peasant boy. The Germans would not suspect that I was a Jew, since they knew that Jews lived in the cities.

After I got permission from my parents to go, with their blessings, I made the journey to the station and boarded a train to Belgrade. The train was filled with grim people, many hanging onto the sides of the railroad cars. I remember nothing else of the train trip to Belgrade. Even less do I remember my return to Krsanje a few weeks later or the second trip to Belgrade with the entire family. I wonder if it was fear that blocked my mem-

ory so completely. I don't remember the goodbyes or the departure, but I do remember that I was responsible for convincing
my parents to return to Belgrade. I gave glowing reports of how
our family members were living in their bombed-out homes. It
was now six months into the occupation of Yugoslavia. The
Germans were setting up shop, so to speak, and it looked like
things might be calming down.

It was I who almost caused a major tragedy by bringing our family to Belgrade in 1941. I wanted to be with the rest of the family.
I somehow expected that wc would go back to holding garden
parties with all of our aunts and uncles and cousins, all seventy or
so of them. How naive! I was too inexperienced to understand the
dangers lurking there. On the other hand, all that happened then,
as always, happens for a reason. We all went to the house where
my grandmother was staying with one of my aunts.

My father was furious with himself for allowing me to convince
him to return to Belgrade, which was full of German soldiers.
He was well known in Belgrade. He had many friends, and he
immediately summoned a few of them to discuss the best way
to protect himself and his family. One of his friends suggested
he hide in the home of a mortician in Arangelovac, which is
between Uzice and Belgrade. Without any hesitation, Father
asked Mother to hire a horse and buggy, called a
"fiaker," and then departed for Arangelovac, leaving the four of
us in Belgrade. He went into hiding that day. Mother agreed to
stay because she believed in the normalization of living conditions under German occupation.

With Father gone, I tried to make some sense out of my life.
My independent spirit and proud Jewish heritage pitted me
against the Germans. I followed the rules published by the
occupying German government. I registered as a Jew and
proudly wore the yellow band with the Star of David that iden-
tified me as a Jew. As a youth of 16, death did not threaten me.
I would show the Germans that we were strong, hard working,

and proud people. Soon the Germans would exploit our pride and diligence to get us together and capture us, like mice in a trap. I, too, would have fallen into the trap, but I escaped because my mother went into action at the appropriate time. She had done it before and she would do it again.

Life in Belgrade appeared normal. I went to work on a labor gang for the German army. We lived at home and every day we reported to the authorities to be dispatched in trucks to our work locations. At first we moved furniture in the German administrative offices. When the railroad tracks destroyed by the Serbian Partisans were restored, we loaded railroad cars with booty taken from Yugoslav army warehouses to be transported to German factories and melted for bullets and bombs. Most of all, I remember the horseshoes. The Yugoslav army had a large cavalry corps and a large stockpile of horseshoes. Our "Jewish Brigade" of laborers, mobilized to do the Germans' dirty work, was loading these horseshoes day after day. They paid us in Yugoslav "dinars" which suggested a degree of normality. I feel ashamed now that I realize that I collaborated with the German authorities by working for them.

One Sunday morning a proclamation went out on the radios, street posters, and newspapers calling for all Jews now working for the Germans to assemble on a city square for briefings. Like sheep, we all met for slaughter, branded with our yellow bands. We lined up in rows from which every fourth person was pulled out and taken to waiting trucks. We were all so naive. Who in his right mind would imagine that the Germans would dismantle a work force that was so cheap and so effective? As the trucks sped away in a cloud of dust, we remained in our places speechless and dumbfounded. No explanations were given for the German action. I was the third counted and my best friend, Nisim, who was the fourth, was taken away. I thought I would get word of his whereabouts by nightfall. Later, those of us who remained were taken to our jobs. Horseshoes, remember? By nightfall we got word through the grapevine from the underground. Those taken from the rows were all killed and buried on a mountain. That was my last day of work.

Mother summoned a horse and buggy again and, armed with some fictitious documents, we got through the German guards surrounding Belgrade and reached Arangelovac. The reason for the German action probably was intended to scare us into continuing to work obediently, but the experience on the Belgrade square had the opposite effect. It finally gave Mother a clear picture of the German intent to destroy us. It dispersed us and sent us into hiding. Our protector was the same mortician that had protected my father. At the age of sixteen, I was not ready to join the Yugoslav underground, but in a way I did go to work for them.

In Arangelovac I learned more about carpentry and painting. The notion of death was not so gruesome to a youth in hiding. I was overjoyed at the chance to make caskets that I later sold to the Germans for their soldiers killed by the Partisans. A good German was a dead German. After all, they were killing the Jewish and Serbian people. They killed my friend Nisim. Now I was making coffins for them. The coffins were all hand made. I cut one piece at a time and assembled each coffin by hand with hammer and nails. Each coffin had to be perfect; the cover had to fit just right. I don't remember if I felt a connection between a coffin and a dead body. I had never seen either one before. But nevertheless, I knew that my coffins were for the dead German soldiers who were my enemies.

I spoke some German and I managed the sales transactions of coffins for our protectors, the mortician and his family. It was revenge! I managed the entire transaction, from manufacturing through delivery. Because I was so openly involved and so natural with the Germans, I thought that we were safe. But after a few months of this existence, the Germans got the word that some Jews were hiding in Arangelovac. In the true tradition of manhunters, they started with a door-to-door search of all houses.

The word got to the landlady who was keeping us in her house and she quickly passed it on to us. She asked my father and mother to take Manon and Leon and go by foot to a neighbor's house in an adjoining village. She told me to go upstairs and get into bed and cover myself from head to toe. No sooner had I done this when I heard footsteps leading to my room. The light steps I recognized as those of the mortician's wife and the heavy ones were those of a German soldier. In those few moments I saw myself in a coffin that I had built, and I saw my parents crying for me, if they survived. The soldier came to the door, with heavy boots and full armor; he kicked it open and, talking loudly in German to the landlady, he asked, "Who is this?" She understood, and answered in broken German, "This is just a little boy. He is sick, so please don't disturb him." As I heard her saying this, I said the one and only Jewish prayer that I remembered. "Shema Israel Adonai Elohenu Adonai Echad. Hear, O Israel, the Lord our God, the Lord is one." As he flicked the trigger of his gun, I again heard the sound of foot-steps. They were getting softer. He was walking away.

My life was spared then, but the agony of fear, escape, hiding, and concentration camps was just beginning. It seems amazing now how matter-of-factly we were all able to deal with the need to stay alive, how innate our drive for survival. Almost instinc-tively, we followed one another. We followed our father and he followed us. The trauma and the realization that we were being hunted in Arangelovac led my mother to return to Belgrade to seek false identification papers so that we could get out of Arangelovac and to an Italian occupied territory of Yugoslavia.

Her transportation was again a fiaker. She was dressed in a black robe with a black veil over her face, resembling a Muslim woman. She asked where the German headquarters were and immediately found the Quartermaster, a German staffer. An interpreter succeeded in convincing the German that Mother was a Muslim and that all she wanted was to be reunited with her family left behind in Salonica, Greece. She was given papers and was allowed to leave without incident. When she returned to Arangelovac, we were all elated. Father and Mother quickly made plans for our departure. Father was a nervous wreck. He grew a beard; his body seemed made of only skin and bones. According to plan, Father left before us again. He thought that if the way was not safe, the women and children would be spared. He went east to Mladenovac, halfway between Arangelovac and Belgrade. The mortician arranged auto transportation. Mother, Manon who was ten, Leon who was thirteen, and I were to meet Father at the Mladenovac railroad station. We were to depart three hours later, without fail. I was very uneasy about the separation. I cried a lot when he left although I knew that we were to meet in a few hours.

When we arrived in Mladenovac, Father was gone. We talked to the stationmaster, all of us in tears, asking about Father's whereabouts. The station master, who was a friend of Father's from Belgrade, said that Father had pleaded with him to put him on a train to the city of Uzice. He had instructed the station master to tell us not to worry but to go to Uzice and look for him in the "refugee" office. He would be expecting us there. The stationmaster was determined to follow my father's instructions. The first train that arrived was a German train full of German soldiers. A woman with a veil and three children would not fit well here, so we had to spend the night at the station. I was in agony. To this day, I don't remember ever crying harder. The uncertainty of ever finding him and the threat of permanent loss were horrifying. The night was long. The wooden benches were hard. The gripping fear of being discovered by the Germans with our false papers and without Father permeated my entire body and mind. Thoroughly soaked in tears, I sobbed continuously. Then, about noon the following day, a passenger train arrived, totally unscheduled — the first passenger train the Germans had allowed on the rails. It was chock full of people in drab clothing, sick and desperate. Men, women, and children were hanging out of every window, lying on the roof and standing on the railroad car steps.

We joined the crowd. Clutching my violin and holding onto the hand rail, I got on. Mother, Manon, and Leon were a step higher. We were all clutching Mother's hands and skirt while trying to hold onto a small valise containing all of our earthly possessions: some clothing and a few books. We were finally on our way to Uzice where we were to meet Father and proceed to our unknown destination; hopefully, to freedom. The train ride turned into a four-hour nightmare. There was no budging from the railroad car steps. Hanging on was a major undertaking. It was cold and windy, yet the expectation of finding Father gave us all the strength of Samson. Finally after a six-hour ride, the magic sound and the name of the town we wanted to reach so badly rang in our ears. Uzice! Uzice! The train stopped. As it did, it almost knocked us off our precarious foothold.

It was seven p.m.-curfew time! By the German edict, everybody had to be off the streets immediately. Hurriedly, the German guards looked through rucksacks and valises. As they came across our books, they asked what kind they were. We had no answers because we were afraid to interact with them. They threw the books on a pile to be burned. We were allowed to move on. We had only a few minutes to find a place in some tavern off the street. We joined the hundreds of people moving toward the town square. Like animals being pursued, we scurried about, searching for shelter to hide from the predators. The shelters were occupied by others who had gotten to them first. Nevertheless, we pushed on. The first tavern we came to had standing room only. The inn keeper accommodated as many as possible just to get them off the street. He knew that people's lives depended on him. The Germans were strict in imposing the curfew and they would shoot if their rules were not obeyed. We pushed on. For some reason of her own, Mother refused to go into that tavern. "No," she said. "Let us move on!"

The next tavern was locked up tight. People were milling all around. "A block up and across the street, there are several places where you can stay," said the innkeeper through the locked gates. "Sorry, sorry, I cannot let you in. There is absolutely no room." Others began to move on in search of places up and across the street. But Mother was adamant. She would not move and continued to plead for entry. A few moments later, when everyone else had left, the innkeeper succumbed to Mother's pleading. He offered to let us in if we did not mind staying outside on a balcony above the courtyard. Without hesitation, she accepted. He led us up the stairs to the balcony.

My anguish over Father's separation from us continued. Finding him in a town where total disorder prevailed seemed an impossible task. The entire town was a refugee center. How would we find Father? Would he have registered, and if so, where? My fears were mounting as I began to settle down for the night. The innkeeper offered us some floor covers and a kind of blanket made out of straw, called an "asura." He also offered to bring us some water and generally tried to make "this old lady" and her children as comfortable as possible. His manner was in the true tradition of Serbian hospitality. As he was leaving to bring us the water, he pleaded with us not to enter the room facing the balcony. He said there was a sick old man who did not want to be disturbed. We acknowledged his request.

But the curiosity of a sixteen-year-old does not take much to be stimulated. "Thou shall not enter the door off the balcony" meant to me: "Thou shall peek into it to see who is there." The door opened when I touched it lightly. I was panic stricken because I did not expect it to open as easily as it did, and the squeaky noise coming from it petrified me. I had disobeyed the request of the nice person who was helping us. Fear and excitement gripped me. As I poked the door just a bit, the crack became wide enough to get a direct view of the bed. Then, as I looked closer, fear and joy mounted in me. First, I saw a patch of white hair showing from under the blanket and then I saw two painted wooden buttons whose paint was peeling on a gray jacket, and then I knew . . .

My father was forty-two years old but his hair was completely white. His clothing consisted of the bare essentials. When he left Arangelovac, he took a coat that had a strap across the back with two buttons. They were painted. Before he left, I noticed that paint was peeling on parts of them and the white wood was visible underneath. The jacket was dark grey. "Mama, this is Tata," I whispered." "No, it cannot be," she replied and closed the door. "But Mama, this is Tata! Tata!" Then she looked and quietly entered the room. She began talking and crying. It was as if God wanted to reunite us. He had led us to my father's door to protect him from self destruction. Father had been prepared to take his own life that day, had we not found him. He had sent the innkeeper to search for us as each train arrived. From then on, I knew that everything that happens, happens for a reason. My fears of permanent separation were laid to rest. Together as a family, I knew we would overcome the agony of war and persecution.

As the years have gone by, some of the details of our "trip to freedom" and our internment by the Italian government have faded. The trip from Uzice to Scopje, in the southern region of Yugoslavia, is not clear to me. I know, however, that we were in Scopje. Scopje had a thriving Jewish community and my father had friends there. We were in Scopje only a day or two. I remember two things that happened there. One was my behavior as a youth who just turned 17 and the other was my lack of awareness that we were still being persecuted. These two contradicting forces almost cost us our lives again. During those few days, I had become acquainted with some young people my age in the neighborhood. Unknown to my parents, I left the room where we were staying to go to a party. There was a girl there who caught my fancy. She was irresistible. Things went fine. We danced to the tunes of popular love songs. We ignored the fact that the Germans might start a roundup of Jews at any moment.

It was a chilly afternoon late in the fall of 1941 when the pall of death fell upon the faces of the Jewish residents of Scopje. The rumor that the Germans were going to round up all Jews became a reality. My parents were in a state of panic. As they were preparing to board a flatbed transport truck to Albania, they realized that I was not there. They went from door to door in the immediate neighborhood risking their lives looking for me. They suspected that I would be in the house with music sounding through the windows. They barged in and grabbed my hand, pulling me away from the embrace of the girl with whom I was dancing. With this action, unbeknownst to me, they gave me another lease on life. We escaped the German roundup by only a few hours. Together as a family of five, we boarded the truck to Tirana, Albania and rode on top of the cargo in the open air. We were saved again by the false papers Mother had obtained from the German staffer in Belgrade. We were all exhausted and very cold. I developed a sinus infection that lasted for several weeks. But we arrived safely.

The city of Tirana, the capital of Albania, was buzzing with activity. The Italians occupied Albania and the entire coastal region of Yugoslavia. Members of the "Camice Nere," the Black Shirt Cadre of the Italian army, were everywhere although there was not much armored equipment on the streets. Tirana was a distribution center for the occupation forces. At last we were out of reach of the German sadists who wanted our blood.

My father soon found a place for us to stay, and he and Mother began to sort things out. The hotel where we were staying was a ramshackle building lacking many years of maintenance. We were all together in one room. We tried to recover from the long truck ride by getting some sleep. Suddenly, several huge rats came to visit us, jumping all the way across the beds, seeming to be having a party. We were shaken out of our deep sleep. This army of rats must be defeated. We mobilized and began a strategic retreat. We grabbed our meager possessions and ran to the street.

Before we left we heard through the grapevine that some of our relatives, aunts and uncles, were interned by the Italian government on the island of Korcula in the Adriatic Sea. Now the dilemma became acute. The travel papers were for Salonica, Greece. Not much news was available from Salonica. Therefore, my parents decided to try to reach Korcula. It would be better, they thought, to be with relatives under Italian occupation than to be alone in Salonica possibly under German occupation. The papers had to be altered showing Korcula as the destination. With that accomplished, Father made arrangements to go to the nearby port city of Durrazo in order to board a small boat to Korcula.

How it all happened, I don't know, but we did board a small commuter boat to Korcula. The crew was Italian and the trip was a short one. We all felt as though we had been delivered from Satan. We were free, but with an uncertain future. The rumors we had heard, that the Italians would not surrender the Jews to the Germans, were only rumors. Mussolini was walking a thin line between the Vatican and Berlin. We had no alternative but to hope that the Vatican would prevail. So we sailed onward to Korcula and to the reunion with the family members thought to be in internment under Italians there. Father felt somewhat more at ease now. There was an air of humanity and civility around the Italians. Even the language was pleasing. The sounds were not harsh even when voices were raised. They sounded more like songs than threats. The Italian language was music to my ears and I learned it quickly.

Our small boat chugged along. All I cared about was arriving in Korcula. After a few friendly exchanges between the crew and my father, who spoke some Italian, I felt a bump and a scissor-like movement. We had arrived at Korcula. The Carabinieri, as the local police were called, were on the scene. They collected the travel papers and allowed everyone to leave.

After a brief inquiry of a few natives, we found my Uncle Aaron and Aunt Elsa. They were living in a small house. We heard of other relatives living with them, but we never saw them. The Italian Carabinieri discovered that our destination on the travel papers had been altered. Soon they were in pursuit of us, as if their empire would collapse if they did not find us. Just as my parents pulled me from the embrace of my friend dancing in Scopje, the Carabinieri grabbed my father and mother. They promptly handcuffed them to each other and escorted us unceremoniously back to the dock and onto the next ship to Split, which was in a part of Yugoslavia that was now occupied by the Italian forces. So much for our visit with relatives on the island of Korcula.

III

INTERNMENT

Split is a beautiful coastal city on the Adriatic coast. I had never been there before. I was amazed at the serenity of the place beneath its brilliant sunlight. Even before the war, I was told, Italian was spoken extensively there. So, not much had really changed since the Italian occupation, except that now the people were answering to the Italian magistrates. Soon we would be doing the same. It was here that our Italian experience began. I always like to call it the period under Italian protective custody.

The swift action by the Carabinieri led us to the "Prefetura," the Italian police station in Split. My father arranged to surrender to the Italians and declare our true identities. Running for our lives was over and we became the wards of Mussolini's military machine. They knew that we were not dangerous to them. They knew that we were out to protect our lives and to prevent our annihilation by the German hordes. We were allowed to stay free in Split. Our handcuffs were removed while we waited to be taken north by train to our place of internment, San Vincenzo de la Fonte, in the foothills of the Italian Alps.

The trip from Split to San Vincenzo was an experience that I shall always remember. At last without fear, I began to feel that there was a chance for my personal survival. Although our family stayed together until we arrived in California, I always felt a responsibility primarily to myself. Perhaps it was selfish, but the time had come for me to wean myself from my parents' protection. Yet, war time was hardly the time to be on my own. With internment looming ahead, all I could hope for was an opportunity to be spared, and then later to experience growing up, to discover myself, and to do something productive. I was still 17 years old and totally unaware of almost everything, except fear and survival. I thought a lot about what it would be like in the internment camp, and how we would be treated there.

We boarded an Italian ship destined for Trieste. Trieste, a city contested by the Italians and the Yugoslavs, was our port of debarkation. We transferred there to a train that took us into the Alps. The adults were handcuffed again. Degrading as this was, I somehow still felt safe. I wonder why? It could have been the mellow manner of speaking or general behavior of the Italians. Their musical language did not conjure or augment ill tidings. It inspired warmth and friendship. In short, it was a promising sound.

The train ride took us through Milan, Turin, and Aosta, and north to San Vincenzo near the Swiss border. This ride, unlike the one to Uzice, filled me with awe. The beauty of the Alps was breathtaking. High green mountains and their valleys were poised to receive white winter coats. The train ran like a clock, powered by electricity from the high tension wires brought in by Mussolini, who had promised the Italian people that he would make the trains run on time. The majestic steel electric towers hovered at times above the valley fog like "angels" in space. Man-made things in Italy, even an Italy at war, were beautiful. To me, their beauty was explosive; the poetic Italian language and perceived benevolence of the Italian people only reinforced it.

When we arrived in San Vincenzo, we discovered that we had been brought to a resort town and that our concentration camp was called "Confine Libero," or Free Confinement. The word free was used correctly. We were free within San Vincenzo de la Fonte. Once a day, the adult population had to report to the office of the Carabinieri. Otherwise, we could do as we pleased. In the midst of a world holocaust, we were allowed to be free! Unbelievable. The Italian government gave us a stipend of 800

Lire per month for support. Out of this, we were just able to pay for our food and lodging. We lived in a two-room apartment heated by a potbelly stove.

Strangely, the entire world was aflame and yet here in Italy people were standing up to the tyranny of Nazi Germany's treatment of the Jews. Albeit, the Italian government did not do this entirely on its own; it could not act without the blessing of the Pope. So it came to pass that all the restrictions and all the inconveniences were tolerated by both Jews and Gentiles under Italian domination. Mussolini and the Black Shirts exercised restraint. They stood up to the incessant German demands for the surrender of all Jews. That is how I learned that all adversities are relative. The adversities that we endured during the Italian experience were minimal because, while the Italians denied us freedom of movement, of expression, and of self-determination, they did not deny us life. The spirit was allowed to be in each of us with restrictions. One denial -- not to interfere with the government -- was accepted gladly. We knew that the war could not last forever. So we endured.

The few things that stand out most in my mind about San Vincenzo were the winter, my father's and my work, and my visits to a door-and-window shop. I remember the cold winter mornings before my father or I lit the fire. The nights were very cold and crisp, but the blankets dispensed by the Italians were wool and kept us warm. The village folks were very kind and friendly. They helped us secure additional food through the black market. Then there were the village idiots. The Italians in the Piemonte were wine makers of renown, but little did they know that alcohol degenerates the brains of babies. There were a number of village folk affected by that degeneration and they became known as the"village idiots," meek and innocuous observers of the society in which they lived.

And then, at last, my desire to meet girls was rekindled. Of the group of about 100 people, there was a family, named Baruch, with two daughters. Zeni was my favorite. Then I met a beautiful Italian girl whose family came to the resort occasionally. She was older than I, but oh, how I longed to be her friend. However, our second class citizen status made this impossible. I turned inward to my work. The stipend was not enough to sustain us. My father and I made up the difference by becoming village purveyors of cut logs for the countless potbelly stoves, the only source of energy for space heating. By hand, we pushed and pulled a long wood cutting saw, clutching onto its handles. Then with axes and wedges we split the logs and carried them to various houses. My mother also helped earn our keep. She had learned English while working for the British Army in Greece during the First World War and gave English lessons to the other internees. We worked one for all and all for one. These sentiments have prevailed with me to this day.

San Vincenzo de la Fonte was the place where I had a chance to dream a little, and like my father, the poet, I too, began to write poetry. Since I was blessed with the spirit of a "here and now" philosophy of life, I managed to be reasonably happy. I enjoyed working hard and sweating a lot, even before hard work and sweat were necessary for my family and me to stay alive. I remember once, in Belgrade, before the war broke out, I came in from a digging job in our back yard to where our entire family gathered around the dining room table about to eat lunch. I had just moved what seemed like a mountain of dirt with a rickety old wheelbarrow. As sweaty as I was, I told my father that I would like to do this kind of work for the rest of my life. My mother replied, "O.K., but only if you study hard in school!" It turned out that I did just what she wanted me to do. I was most comfortable working and learning hard, but underneath all my hard work, the poet lurked. My Greco-Serbian-Jewish heritage packed a wallop of passion in me for everything that I undertook. Later, in America, this passion stood in my way and my father's way. Passionate people and dreamers are not well accepted in a society of doers, yet they are most certainly needed.

Although we did not know it, our sojourn in San Vincenzo was coming to an end. The dark clouds of uncertainty were passing over the village, and we heard rumors on the street that we would have to move. Soon they became real orders from Rome.

I cannot remember exactly the preparations for yet another departure, but the fear of what the destination would be was incredible. We had heard of train rides to gas chambers of the German camps. Would this be our last train ride? What I knew was what I saw: handcuffs and chains. Ice formed in our veins where our blood should have flowed. The same pattern seemed to be repeating itself. We children were left alone, but our parents were shackled to each other. An aura of mystery and silence and hope and prayer filled the air. I remember the train ride, but nothing remains vivid. Perhaps the fear of the unknown is what blocked the details of the ride. But, once again, there was a reason for this train ride. It prevented the Germans from putting their ugly claws into our already badly scarred bodies. It was early in 1942 when we were taken to an Italian camp called Feramonte, south of the coastal town of Cosenza in the Calabria region of southern Italy.

Feramonte was an internment camp and yet it was a haven. I think that the camp had been a military installation. The barracks were long and rectangular. We were able to live together as a family in a tiny part of a barrack and we were allowed to do make shift cooking of our own. It would not be fair to think of this Italian camp as one would think of the extermination camps of Nazi Germany. I know of no one who was executed while in this camp. The prisoners of this camp were called "civilian prisoners of war" and were awarded the same privileges as the military prisoners of war. That condition was a testimony to the Italian people for their humanity. Many people perished on Italian soil as a result of war battles, but I know of no plans or actions undertaken by the Italian government or the Italian people to exterminate the Jews of Italy or of the world.

To this day, I am convinced that all the detention procedures undertaken by the Italian government were only to placate their German partners. Mussolini's illusion of grandeur stopped short of committing atrocities against the Jews. For whatever reason, he spared us, but speculations about some action he might take ranged high and wide. We know that the "Camice Nere" committed many atrocities when fighting in Ethiopia. Stories of dropping live prisoners of war out of airplanes were widely circulated. Atrocities, we knew well, were not uncommon in some elements of the Italian government. The contrast between the German and the Italian treatment of Jews must be recognized as a grand anomaly of the Second World War. However minuscule the reasons that our lives were spared by the Italians, we must consider these reasons a credit to them.

Feramonte meant survival to two thousand people: men, women, and children of all nations, mostly Jews. It meant different things to different people. For me, Feramonte was a place to contemplate, and for just over a year, to come into my own. I had a reasonably good command of Italian by then. Before we left San Vincenzo de la Fonte, I purchased an Italian book designed for those who wanted to teach themselves English. I studied it often and with the help of an Italian-English/English-Italian dictionary, I advanced steadily to where I could understand English fairly well. All the time I was learning, I thought that surely someday English would be very useful to me. I was not wrong.

The climate in Feramonte was tropical. The heat was sometimes unbearable and there was a perpetual infestation of bedbugs that we had to exterminate regularly. We scrubbed the cots with boiled water and soap. We had no pesticides. This twice-weekly pest control was something of a ritual with us. People in the barracks made a social event of the occasion; gossip was born and circulated; rumors about our liberation, the German defeats on the Russian front flew. Oh, how we rooted for

Russian victories. Then, it did not matter what political system should or should not prevail. What mattered was that someone other than the Germans prevail.

Feramonte was a camp where strugglers from all walks of life huddled together, unwillingly, to be sure, but together nonetheless. We were united but very individual. In our prayers, we all hoped for the day when liberation would come, but as with death, we did not know when it would come. So we lived one day at a time, finding comfort in what was at hand. Rumors of allied victories were very soothing. Most of all, before the invasion of Italy by the Allied forces, we loved watching the American bombers flying over our camp on the way to Bari and Taranto. Hundreds of bombers, hundreds and hundreds. We thought that justice was being done. How confused we were. Because our enemies were killing people, we thought we had to kill people. No one thought that killing becomes indiscriminate after a while. Soon, we were brought face to face with this reality. One bright afternoon when hundreds of American bombers were returning to their home base, one escort fighter plane mistakenly took our camp for an Italian army camp. As we all watched gleefully, he descended upon us, in a flash of light it seemed, and strafed the camp. He left nineteen people dead and wounded before disappearing into the sky. I had been leaning against a barrack wall when a burst of machine gun fire drew a straight line in the dirt only two meters ahead of me. I fell to the ground in panic, scraping my back against the stucco wall, a small price to pay for yet another chance on life.

The bombing brought me face to face with the realization that violence begets violence and that two wrongs rarely make a right. Being of a sensitive nature, I was hoping for a better world in which people would derive pleasure from constructive work and not from destructive and ugly acts. I took, again, to writing poetry. My brother Leon found a broken piano and began restoring it. Music became his life's work. Poetry and art remain my love.

As if my poetic expressions had been heard, 1943 was our year of liberation. Unknown to us, the Allied forces had landed in Sicily. We stood dumbfounded observing the convoys of German troops heading north. This time the "finger of God" directed the German armies away from Feramonte. The convoys drove on for days without firing a shot. Miracle of miracles! It was a full retreat. At their heels were the American G.I.s, the British army, and the Palestinian Jewish Brigade-soldiers of many colors and nationalities. It is strange how the joy of liberation overshadows any details of the moment. The war was over for us, but not for the rest of the world. Our joys were laden with confusion. I cannot imagine how my parents felt. We never talked about it. What was there to talk about? We were homeless, penniless, and helpless but we were alive and together.

The camp was now being managed by the American forces, and we were free to come and go. The Allied planes continued their sorties against the common enemies and we watched, but with fear. We remembered all too well the last incident of death and destruction in the camp. One day, when I was just outside the camp, a few fighter planes appeared. I panicked and threw myself on the ground, throwing straw over my head to camouflage myself from the unknown sky machines.

Two months had gone by since our liberation. I began to get restless. The big world was out there and I was not ready to waste my freedom in Feramonte. People were coming and going to and from the cities of Reggio Calabria, Bari and Taranto. I decided to go to the south, to Reggio Calabria. I don't remember how I got there, but I do remember one thing. Along the way I saw a German soldier, dead, with helmet and uniform intact, smashed against barbed wire. I realized how much we had in common; the breath of life, now gone from him, had made him into a victim of war, a human victim instead of a threat. I felt a one-to-one relationship with the cadaver of this man who was once my enemy. I knew nothing about him personally; sadness and relief mingled in me at the sight of him.

My next sortie was bolder. This time, I was drawn to a larger city. I asked my parents to accompany me to Taranto to get me situated. We came to Taranto in a cattle train and eventually found a room where we could stay. Within a day or two, my mother arranged with the British forces in command in Taranto to give me a job as a canteen clerk because I could speak some English. My parents returned to Feramonte, but only after they had instructed my Italian landlady to watch out for me. I had my first taste of being alone and independent; what this meant, of course, was that I had a chance to go to work and earn money. But I was in a state of total confusion. As much as I liked moving on with my life, I wondered if this was what I wanted to do. I wanted to be free, but I detested selling things. I never wanted to be a merchant. My father's drugstore apparently contributed to my aversion to selling things that others made. I wanted my life to be different. My father had said that it would be OK to be a worker and be productive if I also wanted to go to school and learn. So now I was in a quandary. I was working, and yet I did not feel productive. Everything was confused and in flux. While my parents were still in town, I started developing a cold. I was coughing a lot and they began to worry about my health. Yet, nothing could prevent my staying in Taranto, although they wanted me to return with them to Feramonte.

Here now is an incident that has a moral. What happened taught me something that has stayed with me until now and will stay with me for the rest of my life. This incident taught me what it means to be accountable to God; it taught me the fear of God. You have heard this expression before, I know. Believe me, we all pay the price when we disobey the principles of our faith. I almost paid with my life.

I continued working every day although my health was failing fast, and every day I stole money out of the cash register and brought it home. I did this against my better judgment. I knew it was wrong to steal, yet I did it. As a boy of 19, just out of the war, having lived a totally disrupted childhood, I did not know how to deal with this urge. The Italian economy was in a state of chaos. It seemed that everyone was out for himself. I saw people dealing contraband cigarettes and shoes, all stolen from British warehouses. I did not stop to question those acts. It seemed that the adults condoned those dishonest acts on grounds that everything was stolen from us, therefore it was OK for us to steal. No, I did not stop to question anything until one morning I woke up coughing blood. Unable to get up, I summoned my landlady who promptly arranged to take me to an Italian hospital. I lay there for several days waiting to die. Clearly I was not to reap the fruit of my labor because that labor was dishonest. I saw my lips and fingernails turning blue and I could hardly breathe. The Italian hospital was completely out of drugs. I found out later that my sickness was pleurisy. The drug needed to cure me was sulfa. Those were the days before penicillin.

As my condition worsened, I became totally helpless and despondent. Then a miracle took place. Suddenly, my mother's face appeared. I recognized her, but was unable to say a word. Barely opening my eyes, I acknowledged her presence. I saw a guardian angel before me. She sat beside me day and night nursing me. My mother informed the British of my condition. They sent an army ambulance to pick me up and transport me to a British army hospital. Their doctor examined me and decided that I should not be moved. The British then supplied my mother with sulfa drugs in large quantities and recommended that we wait until I became stronger.

At that time the Partisans in Yugoslavia were fighting the Germans and the Allies were stopped at Anzio by the German forces. I was flat on my back. With my mother beside me, I was encouraged to live and I felt safe. The cannon fire lit the sky at night and the Italian nurses, all nuns, prayed just as they had been doing during the last three years. While I had a high temperature and was coughing my lungs out with blood and mucus, I resisted when a nurse took the cross hanging at her side and brought it to my mouth, saying "Bacia la! Bacia la!" "Kiss it! Kiss it!" I remember saying "Io sono Ebreo! Non voglio baciar la!" "I am Jewish. I don't want to kiss it!" I was angry at her insensitivity to my physical state and my religious preference. I know now that she was sincere. I know now that there could be no harm in kissing the cross. Something good could have come from this act, they believed. Then, two weeks later, the ambulance returned and I was transported to a British army hospital.

My stay in the British hospital was my first prolonged exposure to the physical pain and suffering of humans. Sulfa, the miracle drug of the time, saved me while I was in the Italian civilian hospital. Now, I needed rest and relaxation. Unfortunately, my fears and anxieties about contracting tuberculosis were overwhelming and relentless. My cot was placed on a veranda with plenty of fresh air, but in a ward with tuberculosis patients. I suspected that I also had TB and that they were not telling me. To make things worse, the halls were full of Partisan soldiers, badly maimed in the battles in the Yugoslav mountains. Poorly clothed and without shoes, these fighters were brought in on stretchers from boats that came across the Adriatic. Frostbitten feet and bandaged limbs, often only stubs of arms and legs, stuck out from the stretchers. They were crying, moaning, and asking for help as if they wanted God Himself to hear. Some just wanted to die. They were given morphine for pain and treated as help became available. The fragility of the human body was brought to my consciousness for the first time. Though I was fragile myself, I did not know how lucky I was until I saw those dismembered Partisans who fought valiantly for the liberation of Yugoslavia from the hands of Nazi murderers. As I was recovering, I became stronger of mind and spirit, and soon I wanted to move again. But where?

I was brought back to Feramonte. My mother continued her vigil and managed to get eggs and meat for me from neighboring peasants. She felt that I had to have the best of food to insure my recovery. Then, one day in 1944, the news broke that President Roosevelt had opened the way for refugees to immigrate to the United States of America. I remember nothing about the steps required to qualify for this incredible opportunity except that my mother undertook them. She was the survivor. Father was depressed, listless, and uninterested, as if he had lost both faith in himself and hope for a better life elsewhere on this planet.

With the help of the American authorities, Mother located her brother, my uncle Jacques, who had been living in Buffalo, New York since the First World War. This information, together with my recent illness and the fact that there were two minors in our family, contributed to our being selected for immigration to the United States. The assembly area for the immigrants was Lecce, a sleepy Italian town bypassed by the torment of war.

There the waiting seemed to last an eternity. We lived in an Italian villa. My brother Leon had the chance to play on a grand piano accompanying a singer. I roamed aimlessly, enjoying the prospect that we would soon leave for America. In my roaming, I came upon a British officer who engaged me in conversation. Suddenly and for no reason at all that I can recall, he hit me with his whip as if I had been a colonial subject. I didn't dare respond in any way. It mattered not that we were on the same side of the battlefield. The beating by a soldier from the nation soon to be responsible for the demise of the German Wermacht was a sober awakening for me. I realized then that I must be forever vigilant, even among supposed friends. That act helped me understand why our elders were suspicious of our American friends who were soon to bring us to yet another camp, complete with barbed wire, in the city of Oswego, New York.

ABOUT MY EARLY POEMS

Poems written while in internment, in San Vincento
Della Fonte and in Feramonte Internment Camp,
near Regio Calabria, manifest the mixed but pure
emotions of a child in puberty. This child knew
what was wrong and craved for what was right. The
depth of his pain, suffering and hope is engraved in
each and every word to be read by yet another
"beginning" generation.

These poems were written in Cirilik, the Serbijan
Script and were translated into English by
Professor Vasa Mihailovich.

•••••

Like ghosts people
Of a defeated battalion
Are wandering

Women and children
Escaping the beast
Would like to hide
But where?
Wild beasts are all around

Sword is over every Jewish head
Awaiting the orders of the moment
To lunge its sharp edge
On the Jewish people
To destroy the genius and
To destroy us.

Europe is burning, it is in darkness
Screams are heard from end to end
People are crouching and moving
Like shadows
Seeking help to escape Death.

1942 San Vincenzo, Italy

Oh, Moon...

Oh, beautiful Moon,
How dear you are to me!
Looking at you
I dream.

Oh, strewn stars,
How dear you are to me!
Looking at you
I gain in strength

I dream about work,
About progress of mankind,
This is my heart's goal
My genuine goal.

So as I gain in strength
I feel greatly strong
'Cause we shall prevail
Over all idleness.

My tired heart
Is seeking safe haven.
It found it completely
In Riches of Heaven.

1942 San Vincenzo, Italy

In Barbed Wire

They have thrown us in barbed wire,
Women, children, and old folks,
And they torture us slowly like slaves,
They decide what is justice for the Jews.

I am walking endlessly in the same circle,
My walking span is limited,
While far away, beyond the wire,
The charm of the spring is everywhere.

The hot Calabria sun is burning
And the slaves promenade by the wire.
The breeze undulates the tender grass,
While in the shade a duo sings of happiness.

Finally the sun sets, darkness descends,
Always depressing, ugly,
Days are long, nights even longer,
Fringing on something melancholy.

A feeling of enslavement grows in people,
A feeling of abject denigration,
But life still sings songs for them,
Spirit has something that is higher.

They have thrown us in barbed wire,
Women, children, and old folks,
And they torture us slowly like slaves,
They decide what is justice for the Jews.

1943 Feramonte, Italy

Spring

After a fitful night
A serene day dawns,
After a long winter
The spring arrives.

Mornings are fresh, the breeze tender,
And the morning dew opiates with its scent,
Far beyond the hill the sun is rising
While the nightingale trills its song.

Joy and happiness rule the world of the birds,
People in love are awash in merrymaking,
But sadness kills every cheerful thought.

They don't know where their family is suffering,
Winter turns human souls into ice,
And a rare swallow, a harbinger of Spring,
Is worth an entire life for weary people.

In some, serenity begins to awaken,
The spring sun is smiling tenderly,
It bodes the end of the war's tempest,
With a kind smile it soothes our misery.

The consolation is real and proper.
The moment of happiness is dawning on people,
The end of the war is clearly on the horizon,
After a long winter, the spring arrives.

1943 Feramonte, Italy

Salvation

In the middle of our fate's tempest
The hour of liberation has struck.
Send your children to the land of salvation,
Because that is your salvation too.

Age-long suffering of the Jews of the world,
The suffering of the innocent people,
That was the goal of the damned ones,
But through that it awakened love.

Love for the land of tomorrow's happiness,
Love for its radiant sun,
Under which all kinds of fruit ripen
And for which I yearn with all my heart.

I yearn to work in freedom,
For the right of man,
I yearn for an inspired thought,
For the rights of the Jews.

Palestine, the land of our dreams,
Will offer the world an example,
Where people of an iron breed build,
It is our land, our mother.

Hurry, brothers, with joy in your heart,
Hurry to our own home,
The Jews will find salvation there,
Fleeing from the beast.

Hurry, brothers, with joy in your heart,
With pride, proud of our people,
And the beast will fall into the abyss,
The friut of its cruel injustice.

1943 Feramonte, Italy

Declaration of Love

Miriam, a lovely name,
Tender as a flower,
And its bearer
Strolls in my heart.

Attractive figure, beautiful eyes,
The smile of a glorious day,
Tender arms soft as cotton
Or as the scent of lilac.

I love you, my sweetheart,
For you are dear to me.
I think of you endlessly
For you give me strength.

Accept Miriam, in all sincerity
This feeling of mine,
For I am not playing,
This is the state of my heart.

1943 Feramonte, Italy

I Don't Want

The black clouds covered the blue skies,
Covered the Sun, then the Moon and the stars,
While the monotonous rain began to drizzle,
Fatigue and hopelessness are holding sway.

I have fallen in love madly,
I was sincere and faithful,
But now I don't know how
And why I am plagued by sadness.

She doesn't want me, but she is still mine.
To forget her? What is the matter with me?
No! Away from me, you black thought,
You who want to rob me of that colorful flower.

You riding the horse, you cause unfaithful thoughts,
You are at fault, perhaps the depressing weather.
But you won't force me to become unfaithful,
Because my heart is not yet pain-weary.

I won't be discouraged, my friend!
From a bud, hope must unfold into a May rose,
And I will then stroll gay and happy,
I won't be discouraged, my friend!

1943 Feramonte, Italy

New Year

The year has passed
And all the troubles with it.
But an old custom
Must be given its due.

Today's youth, called "Junior,"
That follows new whims and adventures,
Must greet the new year
That promises robust happiness.

And the dance begins.
Girls are here, the boys too,
Everything is proper, festive, wholesome,
The gramophone is playing alluring songs,
Declarations of love, as if from a well.

They are dancing, snacking,
And drinking the ruby wine,
Girls are dancing with passion,
Boys look powerful.

Everything is in order,
And everything is ready,
Awaiting the midnight hour,
And for a passionate kiss
From a girl
To strengthen the heart's voice.

1943 Feramonte, Italy

Rebirth

Cities are suffering, millions perish,
Innocent and guilty are cut down like wheat,
While the liberty bell peals incessantly,
To the sweaty arm of the poor, congratulations.

The decisive battle for justice is raging,
The people, the exhausted poor, are rising
Demanding equality while singing at work,
They want the rose scent and the beauty of May.

They show no concern, see no obstacles before them,
Their suffering has turned into wrath,
They destroy cities and people in their path,
They destroy the old ways that have plagued them.

From the East westward all over the world
Sickle and hammer are the workers' symbol,
The liberty flag rises high above,
The justice of earthly paradise will prevail.

At the end of the "act", the world will recognize
The beauty of unity and freedom of work,
The scent of flowers of the earthly paradise,
Will augur the end of suffering and misery for all.

1943 Feramonte, Italy

IV

FORT ONTARIO,
OSWEGO,
NEW YORK

Almost four years after the occupation of Yugoslavia, we found ourselves in a new country. It was August of 1944. I was almost twenty years old when we became wards of the U.S. government, again in a camp, in the city of Oswego in upstate New York. But this time it was different. We were in a camp prepared by our liberators. They had brought us here to recover from the pains of war, and then they would return us to our native lands. Our parents signed a document agreeing to this.

The four years before my arrival in Oswego had been traumatic, full of hope for survival, bitterness, pain, and resignation, all at once. I wept when nineteen people were killed in the camp Feramonte with its population of 2,000. Yet, at the same time, I felt it was a tiny mistake by our liberators who flew on a mission to bomb the city of Bari in Italy. They killed many more of our enemies in Bari and elsewhere. Oh yes, nineteen dead was a small price to pay for liberation. The resilience of the human spirit is tantamount to the miracle of miracles, life itself. So I endured. My spirit was not to be crushed. I was starting a new life. Life in Oswego was yet another stage of the war for me. To begin with, getting to Oswego was no mean task. It meant traveling across the ocean; it meant getting seasick and being attacked by German submarines; and in the eyes of the American wounded aboard the same ship, it meant special privileges for a small group of war refugees. I somehow knew that I was going to a land where freedom reigns. Some American movies that I had seen as a child in Belgrade suddenly came to the forefront of my mind. An American movie depicting teenagers going through childhood, frolicking and having fun, became real life. I was to be one of them. Charlie Chaplin's movie, "Modern Times," flashed before me. At the time, I understood little of the seriousness lurking behind many of the scenes in those films.

Getting to Oswego and to the newly prepared "concentration camp" for the 982 refugees also meant a train ride from New York's port of entry. Now we were guests of the United States government. We were where we would start our new lives. Mind boggling! Our parents must have felt the tumultuous uncertainty of our situation, but to me and to my peers it meant a new life. That was all. Just a new life: a new set of conditions, opportunities, and objectives to be met.

We went from the ship to the train so fast that my first real glimpse of the United States of America was through the train window. Those were not moving pictures on the screen viewed in a darkened room. Those were real "moving" pictures, as vivid in my mind today as when I first saw them: small houses in neat rows, with streets allowing free access for each owner and his automobile. A dream come true! A house, a street, and a car never meant as much to me as they did at that moment. Each house was painted a different color, each a little different from the others. Who were these people who owned these houses and used these cars, I wondered. Yet, somehow I was not anxious to meet them. I was preoccupied with myself, I guess. To be honest, I don't know what I thought of the Americans except that I trusted them. At last I was not afraid of what was to come. I somehow knew that everything would be OK. I knew that we had been liberated. No one was shackled this time. Our keepers were now our friends.

Finally we arrived in Fort Ontario, on Lake Ontario, in Oswego, New York. The barbed wire fence around our new home meant no more to me than an ordinary fence that I saw through the train window. It merely defined the boundaries of our new home.

I felt at ease, yet curious about the Americans who came to see us at the fence. The questions they were asking were incomprehensible. For example, the kids wanted to know if we had telephones in Europe. Mind you, telephones! I thought to myself, don't they know we are not primitive? These questions were being thrown at us across the chain link fence almost immediately upon our arrival. These Americans from Oswego had no idea of where we came from. It sounded as if they lived in isolation. To them, Europe was a distant land inhabited by strange people. To us, they were provincial in character, but to them we must have seemed strange. We looked ragged, unkempt, and dirty. Small wonder! The saga of our arrival and our circumstance was a mystery made more mysterious by the local press. What they did not know was that we had a history of exile and relocation that went back over 5,000 years, and that the experience in Oswego was but one more repetition of it. This type of thing had happened to the wandering Jews every four generations. Soon, we would adapt to the new climate, to our new neighbors, and to the new country. As usual, the young ones had an easier time of it. Though my English was intelligible, I had my problems. I will never forget the strange expression on a girl's face on the other side of the fence when I told her that I loved her. I meant to say that I liked her.

Nevertheless I braved the English language with a vengeance. I studied it and used it without fear and most of the time the language served me well. I made friends easily and I participated in High School activities. I joined a discussion group and I read English poetry by Longfellow and Hawthorne. Chaucer rang well in my ears. It did not take long before I too started writing poetry. The following three poems were written in Fort Ontario in 1945 when I was 21 years old. Yes, I was hurting for my people and for humanity even then and I never stopped. I questioned the human condition. What else is a suffering Jew to do?

I do not know why...

> *I do not know why*
> *And what the reason is*
> *For somber days I see*
> *And sun looking so shy.*
>
> *Is't something I feel*
> *In depth of my soul*
> *Or the pest, the ill*
> *That looks like a crow?*
> *Or is it the distress*
> *Of millions of men*
> *Pictured before me*
> *As if I was them?*
>
> *Or is it the song*
> *That the spirits sing?*
> *We died for no sake*
> *Man will be the same.*

Jewish people all over the world were in a turmoil. World War II was coming to an end, yet the British "white paper" prevented the Jews from immigrating to Palestine. The survivors of the Holocaust wandered aimlessly across Europe looking for domicile. So they organized and they fought for the right to go to Palestine. The British and the Arabs said no! Ships with refugees from France, Germany, and Italy were sent back to their ports of origin loaded with their "clandestine human cargo" causing more deaths and human suffering.

In 1945 I wrote a poem pouring my heart out.

The Wounded Asks...

And here they come as from the jungle
Proud, strong, and yet defeated,
Humble they are, yet make them tremble
By the name of Israel.

Left to themselves through centuries
They battled through thunder and hail combined
Exposed to millions of villainies
They bravely won the battle of time.

And now as sun's rays are reappearing
And gracious smiles are showing up
Through the millions of wounds still bleeding
A scream is heard of the handicapped.

Is this justice, mankind the free
Called for, this time by the millionth bell
Will this the world of the future be
With no place in it for Israel?

Oswego has left me with many good memories. The people of Oswego were warm and receptive. These sons and daughters of immigrants themselves appreciated what we went through and they probably wondered how can people who have been so oppressed bounce back to a normal existence so quickly. I gave them a reason why with my next poem depicting my passion for humanity. One day a blind pianist performed at a school assembly and inspired me to write the following poem.

On Blindness

The beauty of nature
Its complex, its wonder,
Its color and music
Is subject of hearts.

Yet, he lives in darkness,
Not knowing the world,
Not seeing the color,
The shape of the bird.
Not seeing the beauty
Of the ocean wide,
Nor the smile or temper
Of the happy bride.

Yet, he is living
And doing his part
By giving joyous moments
To those thrilled by art.

The war in Europe was still raging. We listened to the news avidly, wondering when the madness would end. The young adults of high school age were all admitted to attend Oswego High School where our principal, Mr. Faust, dealt ceaselessly and patiently with the high school population. He was proud of us because we were generally good students. I remember those days fondly. The school was clean and warm even on blizzard days when we could scarcely push our way through the wind and blinding snow. Our teachers were all helpful and dedicated to the teaching profession. I learned English quickly. Social studies and wood shop were my favorite subjects, and my woodworking teacher, Mr. Crabtree, was my role model. He was always well dressed, with a starched white shirt, sleeves rolled up to his elbows, and a clean apron; immaculate is perhaps a better word to describe him. I remember his lectures well. Among other things, he predicted a building boom. He inspired us to learn. He said, "From the waist down we all do the same thing, but from the waist up, only those who apply themselves shall succeed." I made beautiful furniture in his class. He taught us how to cut, to shape, and to finish wood to perfection. What he taught me I still remember, as though it were written in my mind with an indelible pencil to last forever.

I was a young man in a hurry, taking extra courses to accelerate my graduation. I annoyed Mr. Faust so much that he stopped me in the corridor one day to ask, "What's the hurry?" My answer was simple: to make up for the four years I had lost in the war. I never heard from him on this subject again! Algebra was not my favorite subject, but I tried my best. Public speaking was another course I enjoyed, and I participated in a public contest. The title of my speech was: "The influence of the U.S. Constitution on the New Immigrant." I memorized and presented the following speech and was elated when I received Honorable Mention Award for my efforts.*

So my speech went, glorifying the Constitution of the United States of America. The work of these visionary leaders, I said, was the foundation of the American sense of justice, liberty and freedom of expression.

Syracuse was not far from Oswego. It was a larger city with an established Jewish community. Some representatives of the Syracuse Jewish community started visiting the Fort Ontario Refugee Shelter. Life began to assume an air of normalcy. Our small apartments, carved out of army barracks, began taking shape. Regular hot showers, though taken in common public facilities, were a welcome convenience that we experienced for the first time in years. No more sponge baths with cold water. Hot and cold running water were the American dream to me, and I am sure that they were to all other refugees. And, oh yes,

* see full text of speech on Page 77.

haircuts for men were also wonderful. I must say with a sense of accomplishment that I personally contributed to this luxury. I became a barber, practicing my trade on a part-time basis. Almost immediately upon our arrival, my father noticed that our hosts provided for almost everything except an in-house barber shop. Since the adults were not allowed to leave the camp, the need for a barber was obvious. So Father went to the chain link fence on the second day after our arrival. He slipped a five-dollar bill, given to him by the Jewish Agency, to a curious visitor and asked him to buy clippers, scissors, and a comb. The trust he placed in this person paid off because the next day the equipment arrived. My father became my guinea pig and I became his. We gave each other haircuts. Then we gave haircuts to all my high school friends for thirty cents a haircut, half the price of what regular barbers were charging in Oswego. My shop was in the public bathroom, not used much during mid-afternoon. From then on, my spending money was no problem.

Belgrade was my birthplace and Oswego was my rebirth place. I was happy "doing my thing". It is sad that my parents could not enjoy the growth and development of their own children. My brother Leon flourished in Oswego. He had his own choir that he conducted tirelessly. He gave many performances in the camp that brought entertainment and joy to the camp residents. My sister Manon, seven years younger than I, had her own set of friends. Her activities in the camp have faded from my memories. Father was the camp pharmacist, and Mother was involved with the Hadassah Organization of America. She taught English and worked in a community kitchen preparing lunches for the students; it was her first opportunity after the liberation to be useful to a community. There were parties, girls, and dancing. Dancing was always my love. To this day, I will dance at the drop of a hat. I guess my Sephardic ancestral passion for rhythm and movement never left me.

There were many visitors to Fort Ontario. I shall never forget

Eleanor Roosevelt's visit. Oh, that was an experience! Then there were carnivals. Our Purim Festival was unforgettable. My mother made many friends. Everyone admired her and her ability to speak English. We met Mr. and Mrs. Sadkin and their daughters. They were to remain lifelong friends.

Then one day we mourned the loss of the man who had brought us to the United States. President Roosevelt's death was a shock to us all. We did not feel that he was shown the repect at his death that a great man should have. We did not even witness a day of national mourning, although there may have been one, and we had no TV then to let us participate in the stately funeral procesion as the president's coffin was borne down Pennsylvania Avenue on a caisson drawn by black horses. He had had many critics because the times were so tense. A Depression had been survived and a devastating war in Europe, but an Asian war raged on. The controversies of Capitalism versus Scialism were at their height. And this great leader had been constantly in the midst of it all. Still, I recognized that in a democacy, government must move continuously along for the sake of its entire people. Thus the new president, Harry Truman took the reins, and would be the one to accept the surrender of the "bad guys" of the Second World War, and what a surrender it was!

Soon, the shortest but happiest episode of our family's war wanderings was about to end – our stay in Fort Ontario. The genius of Albert Einstein, whose discoveries helped create the most awesome weapon ever devised by man, would help to end the war. Although as we were later to learn he opposed the use of the atom bomb, Einstein appeared to me as if God had chosen him, a Jew, a Messiah, so to speak, to warn the world that people must return to righteousness. As always, there would be a price to pay in human life and suffering. Hiroshima and Nagasaki, the unforgettable! I felt that these two cities were sacrificed by God as if to tell the world, "Unless you stop fighting, I shall destroy you all. You have sinned against humanity as I created it, and against me, your God, by turning against each other and by not obeying my laws."

I cannot help but connect the story of Noah with the nuclear bomb. The destruction of Hiroshima and Nagasaki was like Noah's Ark in reverse. This time the people destroyed, not the people saved, were the ones that gave the world another chance. The awesome power of the atom bomb made people stop fighting. During the forty-five years that have passed since the end of the World War II, global conflict has been held at bay. Was the world saved by the atom bomb? Who knows? To us, the residents of Fort Ontario, the war ended after Hiroshima and Nagasaki were destroyed. That was reason enough to sacrifice the two cities. We did not question the morality of the deed. The war was over for us. That was what mattered.

President Truman was to us the epitome of America. He was strong, direct, and common in appearance. He was one of the guys on the block. Now he was the one who would change the commitment made to Congress by President Roosevelt to send us back to our native lands at war's end. It is my belief that Roosevelt had no choice but to make such a commitment at that time. Bigotry was prevalent and it extended all the way to Congress. Not even the most powerful people with humanity and decency in their hearts could prevail upon Congress to open the gates of this country to the millions of Jewish survivors of the Holocaust unless they were to be returned to their native lands after the war. Truman, however, restored our faith in the democracy and compassion of this great land.

We were allowed to make the choice: to return or to stay. My parents decided to stay. That was the beginning of a new chapter in our lives. To me it was the beginning of my adulthood and of my personal growth. We immigrated into the United States as prescribed by law. We traveled to the Canadian side of Niagara Falls, made a U-turn to immigrate into the "land of milk and honey," and became naturalized citizens of the United States of America. The year was 1946. In addition, we were offered the choice of where we would like to live, what city or state. My parents chose California. It was Mother's preference because she loved the sun and the warm climate. Salonica, Greece, her birthplace, is on the Mediterranean coast, and so California was a natural choice to her. The rest of us were happy about the selection and we accepted her decision. The Jewish Agency participated in our relocation, but their financial assistance and guidance were minimal. Our trip to Reseda in Southern California, near Los Angeles, was paid for by the agency, and from then on we were on our own. So, we took yet another train ride, this time across the United States. It was not very memorable for me; I don't know why. I guess because it meant normalcy: coming of age coupled with new perceived responsibilities. Not fear this time, but confusion and doubt filled me.

Fort Ontario Refugee Shelter, 1944.
My father feeding the ducks.

On stage, being a victim in a play.

Not one, but two on my hands.
Left, Sherly; right, Ruth

Portrait of myself, 1944

A visiting Quaker, Miss Klein.
We walked the shore of Lake
Oswego, 1945.

Left, Ruth; right, Sherly. Lots of youthful fun. 1945

With Ruth at the Shelter, just before departure to California. 1946

The Purim Festival at the Shelter.
Everyone in costume. Myself, center, as a Pasha.

V

RESEDA, CALIFORNIA

Reseda, California, was a tiny town in the middle of San Fernando Valley – by nature a desert, now under cultivation for crops. Our family arrived here with only our valises and a few dollars of pocket money provided by the Jewish Family Services, who had paid for our railway tickets. Now they gave us temporary housing in a Jewish Senior Citizens' Home on the outskirts of Reseda – a one story structure with rooms off a central corridor. The stipend offered us was enough to buy groceries until we could find work, and we prepared our meals in the central kitchen.

At last World War II was really over for us. Completely free and on our own, although strangers in a strange land, we were ready to adopt our new country, the United States of America. Josif, Fortuné and their three offspring, Edy 21, Leon 18, and Manon 14, all survivors from a devastated continent, were testing the sweet waters of liberty. Van Nuys Boulevard, a long stretch of paved road with a center divider and tall palm trees, was the main artery that took us back and forth from our lodgings to Van Nuys, North Hollywood and Los Angeles.

Father began work at a Thrifty Drugstore in North Hollywood as a clerk and helper. He was determined to practice the profession he had loved once more – a pharmacist, a man of respect and knowledge. But first he had to pass the State Board examinations and that required intensive study. At Thrifty he did any work that was asked of him, including sweeping, dusting and selling products totally unrelated to pharmacy. In Yugoslavia he had been addressed as "Herr Doktor", the German title which carried even more dignity than the Serbian expression,

"Gospodine Doctore." Now he found the American lack of respect for him as a professional man degrading. Gone was the bow as his name "Gospodine Levic" was not invoked, and gone were the friends who, in turn, had understood the commitment and love he had for his work.

Mother began working at home as a seamstress. She no longer had anyone to give English lessons to, since English as a Second Language was decades away from being readily provided as it is today.

My father saved enough money to buy our first car, a 1937 Buick. Buicks had been considered a real luxury in Yugoslavia, but this one was nine years old and much abused. We selected it together in a used car lot in North Hollywood. In time it proved to be a lemon, and I hated myslef for not being smarter when buying a car, but who knew?

Through my father's contacts and referral, I secured a job at a radio repair shop on Lankershim Boulevard in North Hollywood. I had graduated from the National Radio Institute Correspondence School while at Fort Ontario and could qualify as a radio technician, and this was an era when radio was supreme – television, tape recorders, record players were still in their infancy – but everyone had a radio. The shop was owned by a very likeable Italian man, and we had good luck with Italians. I changed resistors, condensors, ocillataors and tubes, and I picked up and delivered radios for the customers. I drove my employers new car, and I drove it very carefully. However, I had always loved speed, and once when the coast was clear I opened it up to 85 miles per hour just for the thrill of it. But I knew it was the wrong thing to do, and after a few moments I reduced speed and returned safely to the shop with the merchandise I was carrying.

I was laden with the blush of youth, discovering my own sexuality, and I was free just to be myself, happy to be earning some money and happy that the war was finally truly over for me. My brother and sister, I suspect, felt the same way, but we were novices and greenhorns, and none of us could completely benefit from this moment in history: the G.I.s were coming home and we had somehow beat them to it. Our liberators had sent us to their home even before they had returned!

But my father had some vision, and bought a lot in Reseda. Had he kept it he would have made us all rich, because property values soon began to soar in that area as the flat Valley farm land began to be built up in the intense construction boom of the postwar era. Instead his attention shifted to North Hollywood where an old house on Farmdale Avenue was available for purchase, and the money from the sale of the Reseda lot would provide partial payment. Still, it would require an additional $2000 which we did not have, so my father turned our Fort Ontario friends, the Sadkins. Without asking questions the Sadkins loaned my parents the money on faith alone – we had no collateral to offer.

Our ownership of the Reseda lot, however brief, had inspired my thinking about building and designing – forshadowing what would in time become my life's work. Now with an old house to work on I began displaying my natural inclination to improve things I did not like. I remodeled the house using my carpentry skills and innovative ideas, and we all took pleasure in the improvements. My father worked along with me when not studying for his license examination.

In Oswego, contact with my parents had been minimal because of the barrack-like accommodations in the camp. Now we began living in a home like a family. I felt renewed love for my parents, and showed it in my work on the house, and by bringing home a paycheck every week. I was now a man in America, the land of opportunity and freedom. I did not need my parents to protect me, but I needed them to show me love and understanding. I needed to erase the stigma I had never forgotten of being the "ijo malo" (the bad son).

But they were unable to convey the kind of recognition and love I needed. I can see from the perspective of years, now, why this was the case, but at the time it saddened and baffled me. My father was very much a victim of the times; he had gone through the First and Second World Wars and the turmoil of transition from a primitive Old World society to a sophisticated, industrial New World. He suffered tremendous culture shock when he came into this country. Becasue he was a very sensitive man, a thinker, a poet, a pharmacist, a builder and a simply non-money-oriented person, he was not understood. My mother, the person who could truly have supported him, did not. Her intellect was stifled, yet again, and she was emotionally exhausted. She had lost confidence in him – sensing quite correctly that he would never adjust, never overcome the wrenching changes his life contained.

As he saw the children growing up and reaching toward our independence, each in our own way, he felt we were "leaving him", even though we were only going on with our lives as is natural and inevitable. The years to blossom out and begin a new life lay before us. I was full of energy and hope. I expected nothing less than a miracle in my ambition to become my own person. But what should I become? I drove to UCLA to take a night course in psychology – and was that ever a traumatic experience for my father! I had just gotten my driver's license, and driving our newly acquired automobile at night caused him major concern. He and Mother were ever protective and managed to make me feel guilty because I "caused" their worry. They were, in their capacity to produce guilt, typical Jewish parents.

One day when Father was sitting in the back yard reading and studying for his pharmacy exams, he mentioned that carpenters were in demand. Ernest Breur, one of our immigrant friends, told him that he had gotten a job just by walking into the union hall, and was immediately sent to work. So I also went to the union hall where I was questioned briefly about my former construction experience. I told them I had construction experience in the old country, but did not know the names of tools and materials in English, but I assured them I was a hard worker and a quick learner. Lo and behold, I was sent to a job immediately for a contractor building a new house. I had to give up my radio repair work.

My first assignment as a carpenter was to build a job site outhouse. In those days, outhouses were not as sophisticated as they are today. They consisted of a hole in the ground, four walls and a bench seat. My next task was to dig the foundation for the house. While all this was going on, I observed and learned the names of a few things like: two-by-fours, joists, level, building line, and instrument. I felt that I was an expert, and yet, to my great disappointment, at the end of the week, I was laid off.

Clearly I was an apprentice and not a journeyman carpenter as I had claimed to be. I was being paid the journeyman's wage of $1.50 per hour, too much to be paying an apprentice. So, what was I to do: drown in sadness? No, I returned to the union hall the next day and explained that the contractor was impatient. The dispatcher, Mr. Coffey, a compassionate man, said "Son, don't worry. Go to see this man on another job. He will put you to work." I thanked him and off I went. With the knowledge I had gained on the first job, I felt more confident. I was self-assured, I moved more rapidly, and with aplomb I began to display that which I had learned on the first job. After two years of being dispatched from job to job by the local union, I entered the apprentice school sponsored by the union. I did well in school and within a few months, I became a full-fledged journeyman carpenter capable of building a house from the ground up. Foundations, rough framing, exterior and interior finishing, hanging doors, and installing wood trim were all "fun and games" to me.

How I loved the outdoors, the sun and fresh air! Before long, my father joined me. He gave up the drugstore-clerk job and joined the carpenters' union. The next day, we were both sent to work on a tract of homes called Kaiser Community Homes. I loved the white carpenters' overalls. So practical and clean. We were quite a team. We were happy!

Then my father passed his exam, gave up carpentry, and became a California State registered pharmacist. We were so proud of him. Our expectations of a better life were high. We were never to achieve the wealth that seemed attainable then. Even after my father became a registered pharmacist, he still was asked to do menial tasks at the drugstore. Because of this, his depression became worse with time. He continued working for Thrifty Drugs. Later he changed jobs and worked for a small drugstore owned by a pharmacist. He helped me buy a table saw, a jointer, and a band saw, which I still own. Unfortunately, my time to use these tools had not arrived! The military draft laws were still in effect. Of course, we had all applied for our naturalization papers and because of this, my brother Leon and I were immediately drafted into the army. Camp Stoneman in Northern California, near Antioch, was the induction point and basic training was in Fort Lewis, Washington.

The army was a rude awakening to me, and the dream was over. I coped well with the daily chores of the army routine. KP (kitchen patrol) duties did not bother me. The basic military training was rigorous. I was assigned to the 6th Army of the Corps of Engineers and I became somewhat of an expert with the M-1 rifle. I became a marksman. On my days off, I worked in the woodworking hobby shop and fell in love with wood carving so much that one day I caused a minor disaster. At the age of twenty-three, it was easy for a young man in uniform to become attracted to a lady carving a rose in the hobby shop. I completely forgot my KP duty. What awaited me that evening upon my return was a royal beating by two soldiers who had to serve the KP duty in my stead. I was surprised and frightened, but I survived. Experience teaches. The British officer in Lecce had lashed out at me for no reason. At least this time there was a reason.

Drafting us into the Army was a bureaucratic bungle of majestic proportions. The war was over and we had been liberated and brought to the United States out of an internment camp. Now the family was being deprived of two young sons. We thought that something was very wrong. Sure enough, it was. We had been drafted by mistake. The laws clearly prohibited drafting those who had been in camps during the war. This law was brought to our attention by David Levi, an Oswego resident and Holocaust survivor. After the completion of our basic training, my brother and I were honorably discharged with profuse apologies from our commanding officer. At that time we were given our naturalization papers and became US citizens.

When I returned to North Hollywood, I continued working as a carpenter and loved it. I even started getting a few of my own jobs. I built window valances, cabinets, and fences using the tools that my father had bought for me. I learned how to spray-paint and lacquer simply by asking store clerks how to do it. The rest was up to me; experimenting was my love and joy. I refinished a baby grand piano in our garage that I had converted into a shop.

My brother Leon went to UCLA where he studied music. He also took private lessons from famous teachers who recognized his talent. Manon was in Canoga Park High School having her own growing up problems. Father did not understand her, Mother was overprotective, and I was caught in the crossfire. Those were tough but significant and formative times for all of us. I had no peers, no American role models, nothing to guide me to validate my behavior, only criticism from my parents. But nothing could deter me from developing in my own way, and so I did.

The period from 1946, when we first arrived in Reseda, until the time of the establishment of the state of Israel in 1948 was filled for me with meetings and other actions relating to Hashomer Hatsair activities. Hashomer Hatsair, "Young Guardians," was a Jewish Palestinian socialist movement dedicated to establishing socialist Kibbutz life. Leaders of the movement were sent to the United States to organize youth to work for their cause and for the establishment of the State of Israel. Israel needed supplies for its army of freedom fighters—the turmoil leading to its establishment as a state was painful—and we did our share. Shipping arms undercover from the local airports was our assignment. It was a very risky business for a naturalized citizen, but I had no alternative; the arms, rifles, and machine guns we packed were reaching the "illegal" immigrants in the promised land. I decided to make aliyah, to emigrate to Israel. But first I had to fulfill my obligation to my parents.

That was my natural desire and that I did. My father opened his own drugstore on the corner of Lankersham and Collins Street in North Hollywood. He named it Collins Drugs, and soon after that he was called Mr. Collins. I worked hard to set up my father's drugstore. It was a small place, about 25 feet by 30 feet in size. I built a sales counter with 50 drawers with a glass pass-through and all the shelves and cases. I laid the new asbestos tile floor and painted everything. I continued working as a carpenter for some time before my plans were made to go to Hakshara, the training farm where I would prepare for Israeli life.

The camp — administration building

Myself — Barracks, Fort Lewis, Washington in background.

Portrait of Myself — U.S. Army,

Brother Leon — U.S. Army, 1946.

Wood carving I made while at Fort Lewis.

Sister Manon on my Model A runningboard 1947

Mother Fortuné & Sister Manon
in front of our home. 1947.

Father & Mother on front porch of our home.

Father Joe & myself working as carpenters
Kaiser Community Homes —
North Hollywood, 1947.

Sister Manon and Ira, her husband. 1948

Berny, Florence, Sally & Leo
in front of our home. 1948

Mother Fortuné at work in our back yard. 1948

My father in front of Collins Drugstore—corner of Collins & Lankershim Blvd. Completed by me before departing for Israel in 1949.

Our first home, snowman, and first car, 1937 Buick. Snow-covered North Hollywood in 1948. The wild improbability of snow in North Hollywood, was like the improbability of our being there.

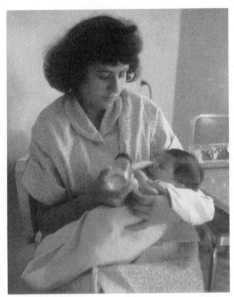 

Sister Manon with her #1 son Ryan David Pollock. Father and his first grandson.

Father at work in backyard.

VI

ON THE ROAD AGAIN

Late in 1948, the time came for me to train at Hakshara. My father seemed to feel that this would be a permanent separation. This is a further manisfestation of my father's feeling of being deserted at every turn, even by adult children.

Traveling then was not as simple as it is today, but I did go. Hakshara was at a farm with sparse accommodations for about forty people in Heitztown, New Jersey. That was where we had the first glimpse of Kibbutz life with its communal living and working, singing and dancing. Most of all, what sustained us was the hope that the freedom fighters of Palestine would succeed. We analyzed every news broadcast and discussed and speculated on the outcome daily.

I was given a construction assignment, rebuilding chicken coops. Heitztown was famous for chicken farming, and the Jewish state would need farmers, workers, and builders. We were all very idealistic, young, and energetic, and work was no chore for any of us. Then the rains came and the windows leaked. I was the "Mumhe" (expert) carpenter. With a caulking gun, not a machine gun, I went into action to seal the cracks in the weather-beaten house in Heitztown. I also worked for a few farmers. One of them hired me to build a new chicken coop of sizable proportions. With the help of a few friends, I made short work of it. I laid out the building, formed the foundations, and framed it within two weeks. To build something on my own with a few sticks and stones was a very exhilarating experience.

Three months passed rapidly. It was time to return to North Hollywood. Yet, I had one more mission to accomplish. I wanted to visit Syracuse, New York, where the Sadkins lived.

The reunion with this wonderful family, who had lent us the money to buy our first house, was warm and friendly. The Sadkins offered me a job remodeling their house. That was a truly marvelous opportunity for me to apply my professional building skills, which I did with passion. I was twenty-four years old and truly a "natural" builder. I was quality and production-oriented. All the subcontractors had a healthy respect for me and they followed my orders faithfully. The work consisted of removing walls, changing stairs, relocating windows, and even installing a new picture window in the living room. All this was going on while the Sadkin family and I lived in the house that was being remodeled.

Manny Sadkin was a generous fellow. He even lent me his car. Once, when I went for a ride with his daughter Shirley and some friends, the car balked. As we were leaving a gas station, a loud noise came from under the car. Soon we learned that the rear axle was out. The car was towed to the mechanic and repaired. There were no recriminations about damage to the car, no criticism and no complaints!

All in all, my stay at the Sadkins was fun, games, work, and earning money. Yes, I repaid my parents' debt of $2,000. I had enough money left over to pay for my bus ticket back to California and to have some spending money in my pocket. I returned to North Hollywood expecting to be greeted and congratulated for my achievement in Syracuse, but I don't remember my parents expressing such sentiments. They seemed to be preoccupied with their health. My mother started having arthritic pains in her hip. My father had had gall bladder problems ever since I could remember, but now the problems were becoming more acute.

I went back to work and study. This time the study of the Hebrew language was most important. I took lessons from a shaliach, a person sent from Israel to organize, recruit, and teach. I learned quickly and was soon able to carry on a conversation. The time for departure to Israel was getting near. The birth pains of the State of Israel were over by the end of 1948. Now preparation for my departure began in earnest. The plan was to go via England, France, and Italy. I saved every cent I could from my carpentry work and established March of 1949 as the departure date. I traveled with friends of mine from the Hashomer Hatsair movement, Hava, Adrian, and Rita. Our departure from Los Angeles by train was tearful. My father cried. I don't remember who else was at the station, but the pain of my father's suffering has stayed with me until this day. It was as if Mladenovac was revisited. This time a deliberate separation from my family was intended to accomplish the reunion with my people in Israel and it was my father's turn to think that the separation would be permanent. I should have known how he felt. But as the train departed, the pain was put aside.

We sailed from New York on the Queen Mary—the "ship of ships" in those days. As with most young people, what counted for me was the present. The train ride and the crossing of the Atlantic were uneventful, with one exception. While we were at sea, the weather did not cooperate. The wind rose into a fierce storm that converted our huge ship into a walnut shell. We were tossed around from side to side and back and forth. Dishes were flying and people were wallowing on the floor with sea sickness. None of us thought we would get out alive. The ship could not enter the harbor at Southampton and it just kept on dodging the skyscraper-size waves for two days. Finally, the crew and passengers were granted a "stay of execution." The storm passed and we docked at Southampton, England. We were greeted by the port authorities with a steak dinner for those who could eat, and cots and blankets for those who just needed rest. Again I was spared and again I was grateful for the miracle bestowed upon me by a higher authority. My sojourn on earth was again extended.

We stayed in England for approximately one week. The stay

was rather sad. We saw the ravages of the second World War. The German dive bombers had not spared one building, it seemed. The German rockets had also done their deed, yet the remarkable spirit of the British people would prevail. London would be rebuilt.

It is hard to imagine getting to France from England without flying or sailing across the channel, but I don't remember doing either. Yet I do remember arriving at the Paris train station. It was a bewildering experience. I had never seen a subway, and suddenly there it was, the Metro. The next thing I remember was visiting my aunt and uncle and two cousins from my mother's side of the family. One cousin was a clothing merchant and the other was a musician. Hava, Adrian, and Rita, who were traveling along, loved me. I was the linguist, always interpreting and translating for them. Big cities have never been my cup of tea, yet the cultural aspects of Paris were great experiences. We visited the Louvre and the Rodin museum. We soon realized that Rodin did not have to go far for his subject matter. Outside the museum, lovers were freely embracing and kissing passionately, as if unaware of any passers-by.

My attachment to Paris and to my maternal cousins and aunt and uncle was not very strong. I made a few chance acquaintances and this helped me refine my native French from my early home life. After two weeks my French became fluent. That was one of my real gifts. Our itinerary called for a visit to Italy: Rome, Venice, Florence, and San Vincenzo de la Fonte, my first internment town in Italy.

We had been treated civilly by our captors in San Vincenzo. The adults only had to report to the Carabinieri and the kids were free to do their things. I loved this shiny Italian resort town, yet, revisited it did not have the same flavor that it had then. Perhaps the springtime changed things. We had been there in the winter, when the smell of smoke from chimneys reminded me of Belgrade. Now, the horse-drawn sleds were gone and the smell of spring replaced the smoke. The factory that had made doors and windows from the most aromatic pine was no longer there. Changes took place quickly after the war. When we were there in the winter of 1941 there were no tourists, but now in 1949, tourists started invading the quietness. The village idiot, who had been a typical sight in the province of Piemonte, was gone too. He was too offensive for the sophisticated tourists from Milan and Rome.

We went on to Venice, where I saw action on the streets in a confrontation between the Italian police representing the Christian Democratic Party—Italy's ruling party—and the Communists. To me, that spelled a fight. Pragmatist that I was, I could not wait to get into the melee. As luck would have it, the Communists turned to another side of the Piazza San Marco, and the police bypassed the restaurant where we were having dinner. I wanted to show them whose side I was on: I was a dyed-in-the-wool socialist, a member of an American labor union with ties to Hashomer Hatsair, the Israeli socialist youth movement. I looked into the reason for the uproar. It must have been the district leader of the Communist party who lead me to the meeting hall. To this day, I cannot believe what I did. Either my youthful stupidity or my passionate conviction that I was doing the right thing led me to make a speech, in Italian, in support of the Italian communists and against the Christian Democrats. As we were leaving the meeting hall, we heard gun fire. We ducked. I had risked my life and my trip to the promised land. I cannot recall the reaction of my traveling companions, but I am sure that they thought I was mad.

We continued to Marseilles where we boarded an Israeli ship for Haifa. My companions no doubt were relieved to see me tag along after my close brush with an unwarranted danger. Sailing the open seas was not new to me. I had crossed the Atlantic twice, to the U.S. and then back again to Europe. I had crossed the Adriatic to the Island of Korcula, and now I was crossing the Mediterranean to the Promised Land. The ship was filled to capacity with passengers from all over Europe. They were mostly people who wanted to settle in Israel and had relatives there, but I was going to a Kibbutz. I had two uncles with whom I could live and I began to be torn. I yearned for family, yet the Kibbutz was my destination. There was much joy, singing, and dancing on the boat by these survivors of the Holocaust and there were tears in their eyes. They had only meager provisions, a valise or two, but much hope that once in the homeland, peace would prevail and reason would permeate the Arab minds. Then suddenly, like a mirage, city lights began to appear on the horizon and we all knew that Eretz Israel was within our reach at last. We all stood up and began to sing the Israeli National Anthem, Hatikvah.

PREPARATION FOR KIBBUTZ COMMUNAL WORK
AND LIVING

Seminars on the challenge.

A trainee preparing for Alia,
"Raising up to Israel"

A trainee at the Farm.

Building a chicken coop. I worked as construction carpenter foreman.

On board the Queen Mary departing New York for England on the way to Israel.
At right: Adrian, Rita (his wife), Hava, and a "Shalia" – an Israeli emissary.

London ruins after WW II

Visiting Aunt, Uncle & Cousin Strumza's in Paris on way to Israel. Myself at left.

Venice, Italy — the Four Musketeers: Adrian, Rita, Hava & myself

Adrian Poskowitz & myself. Rome, Italy

Relaxing with the harmonica on a hillside above Rome, Italy

Venice, Italy. A portrait of myself—young,
fervent, idealistic, ready.

The Four Musketeers — myself, Rita, Adrian
& Hava — skiing in the Alps of Italy.

Myself on skis before departure.
There would not be any skiing in Israel.

VII

ISRAEL, THE PROMISED LAND

At the port of Haifa, a man named Zev Brinner was waiting for us. The Kibbutz Sasa leadership had sent him to receive us and to take us back to the kibbutz. We boarded a truck that took us over roads soaked with Jewish and Arab blood, north through towns that were in the news regularly, and on through Sfat, on Lake Kinneret. The hulls of burned-out war vehicles abandoned by the side of the road reminded us of the reality of war. Sfat, an ancient Jewish town with rabbinical schools, reminded us of the stewardship of all the generations of Jews who had lived there since the destruction of the temple. We had won this land back. We had not taken anything that was not ours by divine decree. Pride swelled in our hearts. With the courage of our ancestors and the strength of our youth, we stood with weapons in our hands ready to defend ourselves and to prove to the world that we would never again be led to gas chambers like sheep to slaughter. Those who chose to live in our midst could do so under the laws of the democratic state of Israel. Sasa was the name of the Arab village deserted by its inhabitants during the war of liberation and it was destined to become the first all-American kibbutz.

Our initial living accommodations were a few stone houses with no electricity or running water. They provided a place for a few pioneers to bunk. We did not care. What mattered was that our work was cut out for us. We were going to build a new settlement that would be an example to the world, a socialist settlement in a free and independent state of Israel. Here, equality and fairness would prevail. The Hashomer Hatsair movement supported the left-wing Socialist Mapam party. There, for the first time, I met people trying to live what they believed and preached. I went by the name David Levi, the name given to me at birth, my grandfather's name that I was intended to carry and to make him proud, although at home I was still "Edi".

Work at the kibbutz was plentiful and varied from day to day. Meetings, directives, and politics of the distribution of labor were daily staples. Many of us did not have a trade. I, the carpenter, and another man named Dudi, who was a plumber and a builder of sorts, were the only ones who did. Dudi was self-taught, hard working, and a leader at the kibbutz. Those without a trade filled in where labor was required. Communal living required services such as laundry, cooking, garbage collection, cleaning and office administration to keep the records for our small army of forty settlers. Of course, cultural activities could not be ignored, so a library was organized in a small stone building down the dirt road. Occasional concerts by Adrian and Avi uplifted the spirits of the one-time city dwellers and college students turned pioneers. Adrian, the violinist who had admired my language abilities in Europe, and Avi, a San Francisco violinist, created the sounds we needed to make the transition to communal living.

While all this had to be managed, security was not being ignored. We were assigned guard duty on a regular basis. Sasa was almost on the Lebanese border. The Christian population of Lebanon was not warlike but it was hungry. Our nightly guard duty consisted of preventing marauders from stealing our cows. The Lebanese never crossed the border while I was on duty, as if they knew that I was a marksman, trained in the American Army.

On May 1, 1949, only a few weeks after our arrival, we celebrated the international workers' holiday. This holiday was important to the Socialist kibbutz movement. So, we packed up a truck and went off to Haifa with our placards, banners, and songs. We made a statement with our presence. The trip was uneventful except that we were all happy. It was a kibbutz-sanctioned outing and it would not happen again soon. There was too much to do on the farm.

The next several months passed quickly. Clearing the land of rocks that had lain there for centuries, untouched, was hard work. Picking up each rock by hand and then carrying them in rubber baskets called *salim* to a central area became tedious and boring. Once the land was cleared, the corner boards for the building lines were put in place. Hopes for new construction and expansion of our kibbutz were also growing. In me, internal happiness mingled with expectations of visiting my family. Uncle Zak lived with Aunt Paula in Jerusalem and Uncle Maurice and Cousin Diko lived in Tel Aviv. I was becoming impatient to visit them.

I approached the leaders to ask for the time and money to make the trip, but they denied my applications for a variety of reasons. Their denials fell hard on me. Perhaps the American settlers did not identify with my needs. My separation and loss of family during the war was an experience uniquely mine. After all, I was an immigrant American whose needs and feelings were not shared by the American-born Jewish settlers.

After I told my uncle Zak about my problem, he sent me some money. The kibbutz granted me time off, and I hitchhiked to my uncle's house in Jerusalem and moved in. There I decided to leave the kibbutz for good. I was torn between joining the army and maintaining my recently acquired American citizenship. After much consideration, I went to work instead for Solel Bone, a major national construction company. They were involved in building new settlements for Jewish immigrants arriving in droves from all over the world. My aunt and uncle lived on the border between old and new Jerusalem, in a stone building where an Arab family had once lived. Across the street was the wall of the old city complete with the Arab sentries and machine gun posts. Why this did not disturb me I do not know now. Perhaps in my quest to be an Israeli, I finally came to terms with the reality of the situation. There was a war, now there was a truce. So what else was new? Israel was an armed camp. It had to be to defend the hard-won autonomy for its people who had been deprived of autonomy for centuries.

Persians, Yemenites, and European Jews were all thrown into the melting pot, much like the immigrants in America. My Hebrew was getting better. I had been in Israel for eight months and Solel Bone asked me to be an instructor for the new immigrants and to train them in building skills. Their work was somewhat primitive. I taught them how to use basic carpentry tools and how to lay out buildings; I taught them to build forms, scaffolds, and roofs. I worked along with them, but I did have opportunities to reflect upon my own life and aspirations. I began questioning and coming in touch with myself. For the first time, I tried to justify some of my shortcomings. I wrote a letter to my father about how I felt about myself and about him and Mother, but it went unanswered. There was not much time to contemplate their silence. I had my life to live, and so I made decisions about how to live it as best I could, intuitively. There was no instruction sheet to follow and no parental admonitions about what I should or should not do to guide me.

I settled into a routine of six days of work and one day of rest. Food was rationed. Meat was available only once a week, but eggs could be obtained on the black market in sufficient quantity to supply a hardworking man's protein requirements. A lunch bucket and white American carpenter's coveralls differentiated me from the other workers. I walked to the truck stop where we were picked up at six o'clock every morning to be driven to work at Shikun Kastel, one of the new developments in the new city of Jerusalem.

I was free to do what I wanted without the dictates of the kibbutz leadership. I rented a room and moved from my uncle's apartment to Rehov Ben Yehuda 36. It was a fourth floor apartment owned by a Yugoslav immigrant, Mr. Yakovlevic, who occupied it with his wife and daughter. It was a pleasant apartment with a view of the city. Renting a room in their home was a real privilege. Things began to fall in place. My job with Solel Bone was satisfying, at least to an extent. Building two-story duplexes was a happy experience for me. I knew that soon the buildings I helped create would house new immigrants from other parts of the world.

On my way to the central pickup point, I walked by many bookstores and, each time, I was attracted to construction books written in English. Though my Hebrew was good colloquially, my writing and reading skills were not. Since the stores were closed early in the morning, I would stop in on my way back home after work. This practice began to make me dream of achieving more in the construction field. I began to challenge my mind by committing myself to learning; I began to think of going full time to a university. That feeling was reinforced after I met a man named Mel Brown in a local laundromat.

Mel Brown was a Jewish visitor from Los Angeles. He was tall and stood out in a crowd. I overheard him talking in broken Hebrew laced with English and I offered to help in his transaction with the laundry attendant, who spoke no English. Mel and I became good friends. I obtained permission from Mr. Yakovlevic for Mel to become my roommate. Since housing accommodations were very limited, he was appreciative of my offer.

Mel was about a year younger than I was, but he was an engineer and a graduate of Texas A & M University. The U.S. Army had sent him to study engineering when he was in the service. I looked up to him and he became my role model. He was a professional and he also worked for Solel Bone, only he worked as a surveyor. He did not have to go to work until later in the morning and a private car picked him up at the house. I realized then that there were greater opportunities open to a professional than to a craftsman, and I started making inquiries about entering a university in the United States. I began to feel that pioneering in Israel was not the best thing for me to be doing at that point in my life. I opted for self-advancement because I saw that with an education I could contribute more to the Israeli society than I could as an average worker. After all, Mel was making a lot more money than I was and, if he wanted, he could contribute more money to the Jewish state.

Still, my dream about settling in Israel was vivid and hard to relinquish. My girlfriend Margalit, my friend Avram, Mel Brown, and I took short trips, "tiulim," and on the longest of these trips we went to Bersheva. I became quite inspired about settling there. I stood in front of the Bersheva city hall, spread my arms in joy, and asked Mel to snap a picture of me. I wanted to remember it should I choose not to settle here.

Bersheva was like a desert. It had only a few houses, but they looked fine to me. They looked like the houses my father and I had built in Los Angeles for Kaiser community homes. The possibilities for building here were limitless. I pictured myself living in a home there that I would build. Then I would be the master of my own destiny. In the end, my urge for self-advancement prevailed over my dream of settling down. I just was not ready. Like a garden variety of fruits and vegetables that cannot be picked before their time, neither could I.

The first National Independence Day, (1950) "Yom Ha-atz Maut," in Jerusalem was a source of great joy and an unforgettable experience. The Israeli army was taking shape. By that time, equipment was coming in from all over the world, but mainly from Rumania, France, Czechoslovakia, and the United States. The courage of our own defense forces and the bravery of the Israeli youth were inextinguishable. Tanks, half-tracks, armed personnel carriers, and the air force were all represented. The flag of the Jewish state showed its colors. We hung out of the windows to see the parade, and what a parade it was. Never again would the Jewish people walk to the gas chambers; they would die fighting before submitting to tyranny and human injustice. My heart trembled with tension, joy, and apprehension all at once because fear of a sudden attack by the Arabs was ever present.

I wrote letters home that again went unanswered. No matter, for the letters I wrote were for me. I wrote about myself, my thoughts and feelings, without fear of being put down. The first year of Israel's independence also became the year of my personal independence. It was the year I started questioning my surroundings and asserting myself in a world that could become better, more competent, more loving, and more caring. I was becoming aware of the man I could be. The kaleidoscope kept turning. Again, I boarded a ship, this time to return to the United States. I had promised myself that I would go to school and become an architect. Margalit, my girlfriend, gave me a bronze medallion on a chain so that I should never forget the words imprinted on it: "Oh Jerusalem, if I forgot thee may my right hand forget its cunning." No, I did not forget Jerusalem, or Margalit but it would be a long time before I could return.

With friend Avi (the violinist) and "Kelef" our pet dog
in front of our quarters.

With Rina, a Canadian member of our Kibutz, and Kelef.

On way to Haifa from Kibutz Sasa.

Banner of Kibutz Sasa.

My first home in Sasa; an abandoned Arab house.

Myself building in Sasa;
American carpenter's coveralls
and Israeli hat.

May Day celebration in front of Haifa railroad station.
The Kibutz population was politically on the left.

Marching through streets of Haifa.
The celebration continued.

Dudi Bainon, the "Mumhe", experienced builder & friend, taking a break.

Kibutzniks working together

Working along with the Druz Arabs.

At work in Sasa, mixing concrete for foundations.

Building settlements in Jerusalem. I am taking the photo of a co-worker.

Single family house with wood roof that I built under contract.

Building settlements. Teaching new immigrants how to build from the ground up.

Back row, sixth from left. I was the American expert "Mumhe". The others are my "Kvutza", the group I was training to be carpenters.

Single and multi-family houses with wood roofs that I built in Shikun (settlement) Kastel.

At work.

A home I had under construction, of native stone against interior wood form, with top concrete tie beam.

Work break with Kurdistani Jewish immigrant.

Yom Ha Atzmaut, 1st Israeli Independence Day Celebration, 1950. The armor signified in our hearts that the Jews shall never again be led to "slaughter" without resistance.

Newly arriving Jewish immigrants from Yemen in tents awaiting permanent housing.

Yemenite Jews learning building trades.

Immigration from Yemen began.
Child care is provided by government.

Opening of the rails from Tel Aviv to Naharija. 1950.

In front of a Bersheva home in the Negev desert. 1951.

With Margalit. Tel Aviv 1951.

Bersheva City Hall; happy with open arms.

Visiting Mount Hertzel.
Jerusalem 1949.

Visiting Telaviv. 1950.

I'm dining with Mel's friend.
Jerusalem 1950.

Mel with friend, same seating,
Jerusalem 1950.

Margalit, my girlfriend, celebrating the opening of rail traffic. Naharija 1951.

Aunt Paula and Uncle Zak. YMCA building in
background. Jerusalem 1951.

Posing with a horse.

The feed was for cows that produced milk, and the horses suffered by comparison.

Building in Sasa had gone on without me.
I was visiting and inspecting their work.

EPILOGUE

I returned to Los Angeles in the summer of 1951 to find more depression at home. Father was not well, and Mother had problems of her own. The drugstore I had helped build was closed. Stories of financial problems and a holdup at gunpoint experienced by my father in the drugstore were awesome. Just think, to survive two world wars and to then get held up by a gunman in your own drugstore in the United States of America! It was a drug theft, and ever since I have been afraid of those who use drugs. This incident contributed more to my father's loss of faith in America than anything else. Yet he was willing to try again, and he opened another store, a space in a large grocery store where he established a pharmacy. It was not the same as Collins' Drugstore. It was cold and impersonal. This episode in his life did not last long and was abandoned soon after my return. In fall 1951, I entered Los Angeles City College and in fall 1953, I transferred to the University of California at Berkeley. Ten years later, after my mother and father had joined me in Berkeley, they moved into a small house that I bought for them at 1357 Addison Street. One day in 1963, three weeks after they moved in, my father turned on himself. He committed suicide by hanging. I loved my father for what he gave me and I loved my mother, who lived to be 91, for what she gave me. They gave me all they had to give. That is all I could expect.

APPENDIX A:
THE FULL TEXT OF THE SPEECH AT THE
STUDENTS' ASSEMBLY OF OSWEGO HIGH SCHOOL

I am not a citizen of the U.S. and yet here I am to speak about the Constitution of this country.

One and a half years is quite a short time, and I remember so well the day the group of 982 people came to the oasis of Ft. Ontario. From all over Europe with different backgrounds and experiences, came people who had actually seen the bloody destructiveness of war. I also know that this was very interesting to the people of Oswego and that the gate of the Fort attracted many Americans who were expecting to see another kind of man; something different, strange, peculiar.

Knowing some English, I listened to the questions posed by the spectators and tried to understand why they were so strange. I remember a girl who asked me "What is your religion?" When I told her I am Jewish, she seemed frightened and said only "Oh, really." already I sensed something that was to complicate the relations between the Americans and me. Another question was: "Did we have telephones over in Europe?" This was evidence of lack of information about the way of living of peoples in other countries. I did not know much about the U.S. myself, and so the mutual ignorance by the masses of people is the best start of misunderstanding, discrimination and finally war.

Now, after having been here for quite a period of time I shall try to consider myself a prospective citizen and express my sincere feelings about this marvelous piece of work, this rock of ages "The Constitution of the United States." which is a solid foundation of the Republic and its effects upon the new citizen.

First, I want to point out that the word "Constitution" means nothing more but the basic law of any association of persons, and therefore I will treat it as such; not as something supernatural and incomparable. There are European Nations with good Constitutions too. Well, then somebody will ask, "What is the reason for so many changes over there? Governments come and go as luggage from train to train." There is only one answer to this question. There can be no successful constitution for any people unless the people itself has a deep and vital sense of constitutional morality, and its essence is a spirit of self restraint which is willing to subordinate the fleeting interest and ardent passions of the living moment to certain fundamental truths which are believed to be permanent. Up to now America has proved the possession of these qualities just mentioned by supporting the Constitution which was so skillfully drafted as to agree with the mentality of men. And naturally, by the sole act of supporting it, the Americans give the new citizen a chance to see the Constitution reflected in their acts and deeds.

Starting with Magna Carta and ending with the Constitution of the U.S., we see the path of freedom leading peoples toward the bettering of local conditions, and the thorny way of generations who sacrificed themselves to improve the relations among men regardless of race, creed or nationality.

In this country's history there were leaders who fought through all their lives to secure justice, promising and actually granting the equality which is guaranteed by the amendments to the Constitution. The thirteenth amendment which tells, and I quote: "Section I, Neither slavery nor involuntary crime whereof the party shall have been duly convicted, shall exist within the U.S. or any place subject to their jurisdiction. Section 2, Congress shall have power to enforce this article by appropriate legislation," is the biggest step made by the government for a just cause.

Let us see what an immigrant expects to find in this country: Nowadays as many centuries ago, we see that different religious persecutions drove citizens from their respective countries, who went wandering in search of more religious freedom. There was another general group who went in search of more material prosperity. After settling in the new world, they had to fight the natural barriers of their development, and obviously, as they came here with the aim of achieving freedom of religion and material prosperity, they strove for it. One of the beginnings was of the Mayflower declaration which shows that the very first immigrants had a sense of union, visualizing it as the god of strength and power. And since the majority of the immigrants were very religious, their setup was somewhat on the religious basis. The Bill of Rights is, if correctly interpreted, a broad interpretation of the Ten Commandments.

To return to the topic I will ask: In what way does the Constitution of the U.S. influence a new citizen and how does it animate him?

To be sincere, I think that most of the new citizens take the Constitution for granted, but nevertheless they are affected by it through the native-born of this country. They see the Constitution in action in the policy of the government through laws that constantly change to address the ever changing way of life and needs of the nation.

The Constitution contributes to the new immigrant the inclination to mold his views about the government and how to behave toward it.

Now in this new age of specialization and creation of destructive weapons, the Americans face a big problem which is : how to prevent suspicion and another war. Does the U.S. want to be alone or would they rather have a hand in preserving an everlasting peace? I think that experience taught the people of this nation that the enemys of successful realization of a lasting peace must be destroyed.

Let me remind you that if everybody is to give a hand to help realize a lasting peace, hatred and bigotry must be uprooted, and discrimination erased from the globe. Consider man a unique creation no matter if he is Negro, Chinese or anything else. He is eligible to enter the contest for peace so long as he has in mind to do the best with it and not undermine it. To achieve this end the new citizen must be approached by all as "brother" and not "foreigner." He came here with high hopes and if well received he will work for it. As to foreign entanglement, I am sure that it does not exist. The time of isolationism is over.

America has always been a symbol of freedom and prosperity. Why should not the whole world have freedom and prosperity?. "All men are created equal" was the cry of those who wanted to be independent. I believe it is still so. Therefore let not America change its ways into ways of behavior that Americans fought against. To prevent it we must eliminate antagonism, through information and knowledge about other nations. If misunderstanding among nations persists, wars will be the result, no matter how many and how good the constitutions nations will have.

EUROPE, 1941
THE SIGNIFICANCE OF YUGOSLAVIA

The memory of World War II is slowly drifting away, along with the warriors who fought it and the civilians who survived it. The nightmare which began in Belgrade for the Levitch family and did not end until New York State in 1945, was only a part of the massive horror, but interestingly enough, a crucial part. Known as the Balkan War, it affected the final outcome decisively.

The German invasion of Russia, called *Operation Barbarossa*, began June 22, 1941, with three axes of attack: the north; the central; the south. The northern attack was toward Leningrad (St Petersberg), the central toward Moscow, and the southern toward the Ukraine, the Crimea, Rostov, and ultimately the oil-fields of the Caucasus Moountains.

But the invasion began five and a half weeks later than its originally planned date. Most historians agree that if the original date of May 15th had been held to, the Germans would have conquered Moscow. Whether this would have led to the ultimate defeat of Russia is arguable, but it would have dealt a devastating blow to the Russians.

The Yugoslav government was under intense pressure from Germany and Italy to join the Rome-Berlin Axis. On March 20, 1941, at the insistence of Yugoslav Prime Minister Cvetkovich, the country reluctantly submitted. But one week later Air Force General Simovich initiated a coup which overthrew the government, caused Regent Paul to flee, followed later by King Peter II. The new government, encouraged by the arrival of the British in Greece, now defied the Germans, denying them access through Yugoslavia to attack Greece and the British.

This infuriated Hitler and led him to mount a Blitzkreig to attack Yugoslavia and Greece. The army he sent numbered

550,000 crack troops with Panzer divisions and the Luftwaffe. On April 6, 1941 the invasion began with such power that the Yugoslav army was defeated in ten days. Luftwaffe dive bombing of Belgrade killed 30,000 Belgrade citizens and caused horrible devastation ... all consistent with the Nazi policy of brutality and cruelty where it met any resistance. It then took only three weeks for the Wermacht to overwhelm Greece and drive out the British forces. The seizure of Crete by German paratroopers capped off this debacle.

But Yugoslav Partisans now rose up and created a severe problem for the Germans. These guerillas under Mikhailovitch and later under Tito were a dangerous threat, one Hitler could neither abide nor ignore. More precious time had to be wasted subduing the Partisans, and even this victory was temporary.

After the Balkan campaign, the German Panzer units badly needed maintenance and repair. These tanks were destined to be used in Field Marshal von Rundstedt's southern attack on Russia. Thus further delay. Even *with* these tanks, the Germans were outnumbered four to one by Russian tanks in the southern sector. Although the German crews and machines were at that time superior in training and technology to the Russians, these were ominous odds. It should be noted that German armor superiority did not last long – the Russians soon reached parity if not superiority.

Meanwhile, *Barbarossa* was delayed by at least six weeks, and ultimately doomed. There were other factors of course, a tangled web which would take too long to describe here and to put into their proper chronology. One of them was German apprehension about the mud conditions on Russian roads after the spring rains. There was only one paved highway in Russia at this time. Another was the release of the Russian Mongolian army to return to defend central Russia after the Japanese withdrew their troops from the Mogolian front for use in their attempted conquest of Asia. (There is a fascinating spy incident related to this troop withdrawal which made it a pivotal event. See *An Instance of Treason:* The Sorgé Incident, by Chalmers Johnson, U.C. Press, 1960's).

Germany was over-optimistic about victory in Russia, and Hitler was indecisive about determining the most important route of attack (which inhibited the Panzer units). An early harsh winter arrived for which German troops were inadequately clothed and equipped. Then there were the seemingly miraculous escapes of Russian armies from encirlement, such as at Slonim, Minsk, Smolensk. And not least was the incredible bravery of the Red Army – losing almost four million men by late December, 1941.

Still, the resistance given by Yugoslavia against overwhelming odds, and its willingness to continue to resist even when apparently crushed, must be counted as a crucial point in Germany's defeat in Russia and its ultimate defeat four years later.

If the Levitch family had stayed in Serbia they could not have survived: Yugoslovia lost 1,700,000 citizens during the duration of World War II – an appalling and saddening statistic. Their escape and subsequent survival can best be described as a miracle.

– Bob Alan Rowe
Berkeley, 1997